G-Men, Gai

MW01296258

The FBI Flying Squad
and the Deaths of Fred and Kate "Ma" Barker

by Brian Hunt

Table of Contents

Preface

Someone doesn't want you to see this.

That was my first thought as I drove by the Bradford house on Lake Weir in 2012. I couldn't even glimpse the two-story lake house from the road. As I drove east on County Road 25, hugging the north shore of the lake, tidy yards and fences lined the road. The cabins and houses weren't big, but people clearly had a pride of ownership. And then the Bradford property loomed up like a leafy tsunami. Vines and bushes erupted from the ditch in unkempt swirls. A thick 10-foot wall of foliage blocked out sunlight for the length of the property line.

This place hasn't just been let go, I thought. It wants to be forgotten.

I wanted to see the house where Ma and Fred Barker met their fates in a famous 1935 shootout with the FBI. I was researching a story about the events that led up to that day. Pulling my car over on the gravel side of the road, I peered through a gap in the bushes. Faded and water-stained *PRIVATE PROPERTY* and *NO TRESPASSING* signs were nailed to nearby trees. I could see the wood clapboard siding of the house and not much more. Part of me expected someone with a shotgun to appear and ask me to leave.

At some point in the past, there had been a lot of curiosity seekers. Immediately after the shootout, the Bradford family had charged $0.50 for the curious to traipse through the house. As the gangster era ended and World War II transformed the country, the house was forgotten. Toward the end of the twentieth century, nostalgia returned. The Lake Weir Chamber of Commerce staged annual reenactments of the shootout on "Ma Barker Day." Tommy gun toting G-men stood on the running boards of antique cars as they raced into town. A replica of the Bradford house had been reconstructed like a Hollywood prop, a façade of wood and plaster connected to a trailer and wheeled into an open lot. The G-Men stopped their cars and surrounded the house. One honorary person got to play lead FBI agent E.J. Connelley (remembered as C.F. Connally – the historical details were fuzzy) as he walked up to the front door and called out his apocryphal words, "Ma and Fred Barker, come on out. It's the FBI. We've got the house surrounded." A local mother and son got to play the Barkers and utter their lines, "Let's see what Freddie has to say about that." Blank cartridges popped and exploded for a few minutes as onlookers cheered. The performance was repeated two more times later in the day, with picnics and other activities in between the reenactments.

But the legend lost its luster. The reenactments stopped in 2006.

The house languished.   Now, people like myself were more of a nuisance than anything. *You trotting out that old tired saw about Ma Barker?* I imagined a local telling me.   The place carried that forlorn feeling.   I got back into my car and drove away.   What had really happened that day?   Who were the FBI agents who risked their lives? How did they track down the Barker gang to this small house in the middle of nowhere Florida?

The tangle of overgrowth protecting the Bradford property from the road kept creeping back into my mind.   The Barkers were dead. The agents who participated in the raid were dead.   The town had stopped celebrating its' own history.

The past just wants to be forgotten.

PART I - THE INVESTIGATION

Chapter 1 - THE G-MEN

Special Agents in Charge, FBI, circa 1935

J. Edgar Hoover's "G-Men" were famous.

As the Great Depression deepened and crime erupted in the Midwest, the Special Agents of the Division of Investigation were the perfect antidote. College boys, Boy Scouts, call them what you wanted. The fedora and snappy suit wearing federal men became identified with the scientific movement in law enforcement and they were getting results.

Fresh off his success in cornering John Dillinger, Melvin Purvis was *the* star. But trouble was brewing inside the Bureau. Purvis had become a celebrity, more popular in the public's eye than Hoover himself. Looking past the handshakes and smiles captured in press photographs, Hoover had not been pleased with Purvis' management of the Chicago office. Many accounts attribute this to Hoover's dislike of Purvis' fame.

While true to some extent, FBI files show Purvis poor performance was also to blame. However well liked he was by the public or those who worked for him, Purvis made critical errors: he arrested the wrong suspects in the Hamm kidnapping, he missed a chance to capture Machine Gun Kelly, he blew the raid at Little Bohemia (civilians were wounded and agent Carter Baum died), and the Dillinger hunt was an embarrassing fiasco that ended in a public execution with innocent citizens standing several feet away from the fatal shots.

Hoover's memos to Purvis were clear he was out of his league leading a law enforcement unit. His reports were not as detailed as other agents, he failed to make underworld contacts that might provide leads. Men were killed under Purvis' leadership.

Purvis was either blinded by his friendship with the press or he knowingly tolerated leaks within his office. Chicago newspapers knew things that only those inside the Chicago FBI office knew. This infuriated Hoover. The Director had shown with SAC Wener Hanni in St. Paul that he would replace a SAC without hesitation. With Dillinger and Pretty Boy Floyd off the list of public enemies, attention turned to those remaining: Baby Face Nelson, Fred Barker, Alvin Karpis, Doc Barker, and Harry Campbell.

Morale in the Chicago office was low. The Dillinger and Barker-Karpis cases demanded long hours of investigation, month after month. The people in the office felt like outsiders, that Washington had usurped their power. For a brief moment, spirits lifted in late November when they heard that Sam Cowley and Herman Hollis had found Baby Face Nelson in Barrington, Illinois. But the entire news was bad – both Hollis and Cowley had been shot by Nelson and died. Nelson was still on the loose (his body would be found days later).

Hoover privately mourned the loss of one his best men. In some respects, Hoover considered Sam Cowley more responsible for the apprehension of John Dillinger than Purvis (though they had worked together). This was not exactly true – Hoover would provide Cowley additional credit after he and Purvis fell out. Ultimately, though, leading into the winter of 1934 Hoover did not want to let the task of finding the Barker-Karpis gang fall back into Purvis's hands. So instead he planned his next step.

Earl "E.J." Connelley spoke at the Buckeye State Sheriff's Association in Columbus, Ohio in early December, 1934. Connelley was an Irish Catholic who'd grown up in a working class family, the oldest of nine children. During World War I, he managed the Army Signal Corps depot on Bedloe's Island. After studying law and accounting in New York, he became a Special Agent in the Bureau of Investigation in 1920. Connelley earned J. Edgar Hoover's trust and worked his way up the chain of command over 14 years. His positions included Special Agent in Charge (SAC) in Seattle, St. Louis, New York, and Cincinnati.

It isn't noted how he exactly received word, but it's likely that after finishing his speech, he was handed a telegram from the Director.

It was an urgent request - report to Chicago immediately. Connelley barely had time to return home to Cincinnati and say goodbye to his wife and son. The weight of Sam Cowley and Herman Hollis's deaths and the pressure of Hoover's expectations hung on his shoulders as he rode the train toward Chicago. He had no idea that the most intense period of his professional was about to hit him like an earthquake.

On December 6, 1934, Hoover sent a confidential memo to all FBI offices:

> "E.J. Connelley has been placed in charge of the investigations of the above entitled cases and is maintaining an office in the New York Life Insurance Building."[1]

The "above entitled cases" were the Bureau's most pressing: the unresolved leads of Dillinger case, the Kansas City Massacre, and the Barker-Karpis gang and their kidnappings of William Hamm and Edward Bremer.

In a move that effectively cut off Purvis and the rest of the Chicago office, Connelley set up a separate office in Chicago in the New York Life building. While those in the existing Chicago office saw this as a move to excise them from the action, it had practical purposes. Connelley and his squad could operate away from the influence of reporters and others entrenched in the office. It also gave him anonymity that he relished. "I do not believe it desirable that I disclose my identity here," he wrote to Hoover.[1]

He inherited a mess. The Bremer kidnapping file, at its conclusion, would contain tens of thousands of memos, reports, and letters. Agents worked furiously to track down leads, interviewing and watching family members and associates of the Barker gang. Nothing productive was happening and Connelley knew he was up against the wall. Like Purvis, if he didn't get results, the favoritism Hoover had displayed would disappear.

Hoover delineated Connelley's "exclusive jurisdiction" over JODIL, BREKID, and the Kansas City Massacre, and Stollnap. "It is to be distinctly understood," Hoover wrote Tamm, "that at any time when Mr. Connelley needs additional aid or assistance of any character from the regular Chicago office, all that he will have to do will be to communicate with Mr. Purvis, and Mr. Purvis should be under orders to promptly comply with Mr. Connelley's request."[2] Hoover sent letters both to Connelley and Purvis and required them to reply their understanding by letter. Connelley had to make due with the agents already assigned to him.

The Dillinger squad had been assembled by Hoover himself. Hoover recruited Texas and Oklahoma law men, who were just as good of shots as they were police men, to counter the gun violence of the criminals they were chasing. While somewhat disbanded following Dillinger's death, certain men remained on duty. Connelley scanned the roster. Some of the men he had worked with previously. Others were well known within the Bureau. Charles Winstead was one of the agents credited with firing the shot that killed John Dillinger. James "Doc" White was a former Texas Ranger who had joined the Bureau in 1924; his skill with a shotgun and machine gun were well known. McDade. Sullivan. Campbell. He read the prior inspection reports to get a feel for the men's efficiency ratings and evaluations.

Connelley tried to signal a change in how the Bureau was handling itself in Chicago. Gone was the soft, diplomatic, easy-going style of Melvin Purvis. After an incident where a U.S. Marshal let a newspaper reporter interview an informant, Connelley told Hoover not to register a formal complaint with the U.S. Attorney as it would damage their cooperation with Bureau agents. It wouldn't happen again, Connelley told Hoover. The U.S. Attorney's office in Chicago was "sufficiently frightened" after Connelley "very forcibly indicated to them his displeasure at this occurrence."[3]

Connelley hadn't worked a lot on BREKID, the $200,000 kidnapping of Edward Bremer in St. Paul, Minn. But he knew all about the gang that was involved. He studied the case file, photos of the criminals and their girlfriends and associates, and worked to put together the disparate leads.

As the bitter cold of winter descended on the Midwest, Connelley worked all hours to try and manage a case that was the biggest challenge of his career.

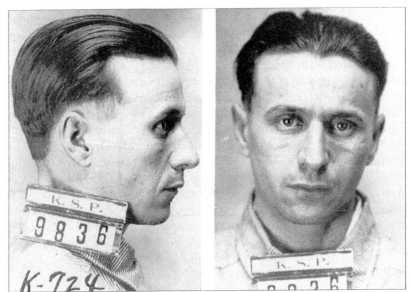

Fred Barker, 1927, courtesy FBI

The Barker-Karpis gang had slowly disbanded following the release of Edward Bremer. The kidnapping occurred on January 16, 1934. Bremer was on his way to work at the Commercial State Bank, where he was the president. His father, Adolph Bremer, also owned Schmidt brewery. Publicly, the business stayed afloat during Prohibition by making "near-beer." Privately, Bremer was rumored to have supplied gangsters, bootleggers, and politicians with a healthy supply of the good stuff. This was St. Paul, after all, and superficial appearances of propriety had to be maintained. But now that the Volstead Act had been repealed, Adolph cut ties with the bootleggers who had kept him in business. He was a target.

The morning of the kidnapping, Adolph's son followed his usual routine. Then, stopping him on the sidewalk, Doc Barker (one of four hoodlums born to Kate 'Ma' Barker) punched and pistoled whipped Edward Bremer to coerce him into getting into their car. They took him to Illinois to wait out the ransom negotiations. Then, after collecting a $200,000 ransom, the gang released Bremer on February 7th.

Fred Barker and Alvin Karpis laid low in the following months and escaped arrest as they moved from Chicago to Toledo to Cleveland. Fred Barker was born in 1902, the youngest son of Arizona "Kate" and George Barker. His father worked in various jobs as a farmer, watchmen, station engineer, and clerk.[04] Fred grew up in Tulsa,

Oklahoma, running the streets with the Central Park Gang, whose members included his older brothers Herman, Lloyd, and Arthur "Doc" Barker, Volney Davis, and Harry Campbell. The gang of young toughs committed various burglaries and robberies in Missouri, Kansas, and Oklahoma. One burglary in Okmulgee ended in a gunfight that wounded, and later killed, a police captain. Fred robbed a bank in Winfield, Kansas, was arrested, and went to the Kansas State Prison on March 12, 1927.

Instead of reforming him, prison served as a catalyst for further crime. It was there Fred met Alvin Karpis and the Barker-Karpis gang was formed. Six years younger than Barker, Karpis was intelligent, brash, and dangerous. He meticulously planned burglaries, mapped out escape routes, wrote down the mileage of each turn, and stashed cans of gasoline along the roads for emergency use. If there was a "brains" to the gang, it was Karpis. Regarding Barker he later said, "Freddie had a vicious streak. To be frank, I was sometimes slightly stunned by Freddie's free and easy way with a gun. He never seemed to mind gunning down anybody who stood in his way, whether it was a cop, or a hood, or an ordinary guy on the street."[5] For all of Karpis' cool calculation, Fred Barker had a violent temper, was hotheaded and quick to lash out.

In four years time, the Barker-Karpis gang stole and ransomed over $1,000,000 - $15,000,000 in today's valuation.

Fred Barker's wanted poster from October 11, 1934 indicates he went by multiple aliases, including the surname Blackburn. His mutilated fingerprints were on file with the Bureau and circulated to law enforcement across the country. In the mug shot, Barker stared at the camera with a look of bored defiance. The first few inches of sand-brown hair above his ears and neck were shaved; the rest was slicked back on his head with Vaseline Hair Tonic. If you met him on the street, you might mistake him for a teenager: 5'4", 115 pounds. Two of his upper front teeth and one lower tooth were capped in gold.[6]

On September 6th, 1934, the gang received a tip that their house in Toledo was going to be raided. As police waited down the street from their bungalow in preparation, Fred and Doc Barker, Alvin Karpis, and Harry Campbell packed up their belongings. Their underworld contacts had been tipped about the impending raid; the city had grown too "hot" for them to stay. They escaped to Chicago and split up their Bremer ransom money and weapons.

Barker and Karpis probably had a conversation similar to one that had occurred earlier in March:

Fred Barker asked, "Where do you think we ought to go?"
"Well, what do you mean by we, now?" Karpis said. "Just who

is we?"

"Well," Barker said, "Ma and me and you."

"No, not Ma," Karpis replied. "She ain't going with us, Freddie. I've told you this before. She's gonna get you killed. Mark my words."[7]

There was a deep connection between Kate "Ma" Barker and her son Fred. Rumors swirled that he could not keep a steady girlfriend (even at age 32) because she always ran them off. Though no evidence has ever been uncovered she was involved in planning or executing any crime, stories abound about her fierce protection of her favorite son. And apparently, Fred did not see a future where he traveled without her. Until things cooled off with law enforcement, Karpis and his pregnant girlfriend were heading to Cuba, and could be reached through the manager at the El Comodoro Hotel in Miami. The Barkers would remain in Chicago and figure out where they would go next. Barker and Karpis, who had been together since 1931, said their goodbyes.

Doc Barker stayed in Chicago. Fred and Ma decided they were going down to Florida as well. It was winter and the weather would be much more pleasant while they waited out the police attention.

Bradford House, Ocklawaha FL, courtesy FBI

Carson Bradford built himself a nice winter home in 1931. The Nashville, Tennessee native had arrived in Miami in 1921 and along with his father, operated the Bradford Amusement Company. They built a $500,000 theater, the Fairfax, the first of its kind in south Florida. When the tropical heat became too much, he could drive north to Lake Weir and seek respite in cooler temperatures by the lake.

Ocklawaha, Weirsdale, and the surrounding area were citrus country. After a wave of freezes sent farmers further south, many sought refuge near lakes, where it was believed the water would moderate the effect of any future freezing temperatures. The rolling hills filled with the wide canopies of orange, lemon, and grapefruit trees. Ocklawaha itself was nothing more than a little village, with a post office, a gas station, and a collection of lake houses. It was nine miles east of the main north-south highway that bisected the state.

Bradford's two-story frame house, the "Belle Air," had white clapboard siding and green trim, four bedrooms with pine floors upstairs, hardwood floors downstairs, and a chimney in the living room for those cool Florida winter nights. The walls and ceiling were made of the new plaster of Paris composition called "sheet rock." The property had mature live oaks, pine, and a grove of orange trees. The best feature of the house was a screened porch that looked out on a 100-yard wooden sidewalk that led to a dock, boathouse, and the wide

15

expanse of the lake. Cypress trees jutted up from the water's edge, surrounded at their roots by thick stands of saw grass and white sand beach. A perfect place for rest, fishing, and relaxation. It had cost him seven thousand dollars to build, and was worth every penny for the leisure it afforded.[8]

In early November 1934, Joe Adams telephoned him. Bradford had known Adams for the last 16 years; the 6'1" man cut a tall figure in any crowd and was the manager of the El Comodoro Hotel in Miami. They interacted at the Biscayne Kennel Club, a dog track that Bradford had 10% ownership in and was its publicity man. They'd first met in Tennessee when Bradford was starting his "show business."[9]

Adams had some friends in town, the Blackburns, an elderly woman and her two sons that had made several trips around the state and were planning on renting a lake home around Orlando. Knowing Bradford had a place near there in Ocklawaha, he wanted to know if Bradford would rent his house. Adams had already showed his friends on a road map where it was, they'd driven up and looked it over and were interested.

I've never rented the house before, Carson Bradford said.

These friends of mine are willing to pay $75 to $100 a month for it.

Bradford seemed surprised at the amount. At the time, the cottage next to the main house was renting for $8 a month. $75 to $100? He couldn't turn such a deal down.

Adams asked, How many months can they use the house?

At that rate, however long they wanted.

So the Blackburns – Ma Barker, Fred Barker, and Harry Campbell - through Adams, paid the first and last month of the rent in advance, $150.00. It was paid in cash with three $50 bills from the Bremer ransom money. Bradford never saw the renters; no lease was created. He knew Joe Adams vouched for these people, and that was good enough for him.[10]

The Barkers hired a bellhop at the El Comodoro Hotel, William Johnson, to drive them up to the house and work as their caretaker. The group checked out on November 7th and Johnson drove them in their 1934 Buick coupe up to Bradford's lake house. Johnson said the Barkers were "quiet and frugal with their money" and seemed like ordinary people. But they were only paying $10 a week. He could make more than that in Miami at the hotel. After two weeks, he quit and went back to Miami to get his job back at the hotel. But as a final favor, Fred Barker gave Johnson $10 to purchase the Miami daily newspapers and forward them to Oklawaha for him.[11] This was documented by a telegram that Adams sent to Fred Barker, indicating that along with the newspapers he was sending him new license plates to use for his car:

MIAMI FLO NOV 21 1934

T C BLACKBURN
CARSON BRADFORD HOME OCKLAWAHA FLO

I HAVE BEEN SICK STOP PAPERS WILL START TODAY SORRY OF DELAY STOP MAILING PLATES TODAY STOP THANKS FOR THE FISH DID ENJOY THEM SO MUCH STOP REGARDS TO ALL

MONROE ADAMS[12]

Neighbors immediately took note of the visitors. Frank Barber kept an eye on the Bradford property while it was vacant, unless Carson Bradford sent a friend to stay there, or the times Bradford or his parents arrived. But when Barber came home from work one night, his wife told him that an automobile had pulled in to the neighboring house. Two young men, an older woman, and a Negro chauffeur. Barber looked through the trees across the lane in the dark. Lights were on in the house and garage. In subsequent days he talked to them and tried to get to know his new neighbors.

Do you have any interest in the Miami dog tracks Mr. Bradford owns?

I don't, Fred Barker said, but "Ma" does.[13]

Joe Adams came up to the Bradford home from time to time to visit them, so Barber assumed these men ran with Bradford and the dog track crowd.

Another neighbor, Mrs. Westberry, lived in a home near the Barbers, just off a lane to the east of the Bradford house. Her husband was frequently gone during the week, leaving her idle time to spend with her daughter. The new people that had rented out the Bradford place "acted rather queerly." For starters, the husband seemed about thirty years younger than his wife, who was old enough to be his mother. Whenever Mrs. Westberry had somebody over to her house, she noticed that her new neighbors would watch them to see who they were. Nearly every morning, the old woman would come out the front door of her house and walk to the garage, which sat between the two houses, and stand at the corner and look over the Westberry house. She would walk around the house and then return to her own.[14]

And then there was the other man with them, George Summers (Harry Campbell). Mrs. Westberry did not care for Wynona Burdette, the woman who Campbell brought back with him a few weeks later. She described her "as tall and slender, about twenty years of age, dark hair which was a rather long bob, curled on the ends in the back, was rather flashily dressed and walked with a haughty manner, smoked cigarettes incessantly and would appear each and every day with a different dress and coat on."[15]

Among all their odd behavior, they always kept their lights on in the garage at night. When Mr. Westberry came home on the weekends and arrived late at night and drove down the lane, Fred and Harry would be out there in the yard or near the garage, shining a flashlight on him.[16]

The Sextons rented the small cottage on the Bradford property for $8 a month. Their three children could play at the lake and they were only 12 miles from Ocala, where Mr. Sexton worked for the Fire Department. Everything seemed to be going well until the Barkers arrived that November. They shot rifles off the dock practically every day and even at night. Harry Campbell sat in his Ford V-8 coupe every afternoon in front of the house with a rifle, like he was guarding the place. A Philco radio blared police reports and music loud enough for the neighbors to hear.

One day (before he had gone to Oklahoma to get Wynona) Campbell drove his car over to the edge of the Sexton's porch. Mr. Sexton was gone at work.

Campbell was a handsome man, with an easy charm. Do you object to me coming over? he asked.

I don't mind, she said. I enjoy the radio.

Campbell then drove her to the Ocklawaha Inn where they had dinner. He started paying a lot of attention to her. He gave her a case of liquor and insisted she drink with him. She refused. Later he brought beer, figuring it was lighter fare she was interested in. Campbell "propositioned" her, a euphemism of the era for asking her to have sex with him. When she turned him down, Campbell told her he wanted her to move out of the cottage. He wanted a woman living there who would be amenable to such a "proposition."[17]

The Barkers used a dispute over getting water from the Bradford house to evict the Sextons. Barker called Joe Adams. The Sextons "were annoying them" and they wanted Mr. Bradford to make them leave. On December 3rd, Marian Bradford mailed the Sextons a notice to vacate the premises at once. They packed up their belongings and left.[18]

After William Johnson left, the gang hired Willie Woodbury to work as a cook, handyman, and caretaker for $20 a month. Woodbury and his wife took up residence in the now-empty Sexton cottage. He got

18

to know their habits and preferences. Fred Barker took up in the southwest bedroom upstairs, his mother in the northwest, and Harry Campbell took up in the northeast room.

Fred had a .33 caliber rifle, a .22 automatic rifle (which he referred to as his "Big Bertha"), and two shotguns that he took out in the motorboat on the lake from time to time to hunt geese and ducks. He seemed to favor the .33, carrying it with him in the evening. But Woodbury could never get a closer look at the firearms - the closet in Barker's bedroom was always locked.[19]

Campbell left for several days in December and returned with Wynona Burdette. She received a Chicago daily newspaper, sent up Adams' hotel in Miami. Part of Woodbury's duty every evening was to gather all the newspapers in the house and burn them in the fireplace.

Campbell drank heavily and continuously while at the house. Woodbury observed his movements as "characteristically slow and lazy-like and he was always running his fingers through his hair."[20]

Overall for the Barkers, things couldn't have been better. Their aliases had kept them incognito and Harry Campbell was behaving himself. The hunting and fishing were excellent, just as good as it had been in Minnesota. Fred and Harry liked to go out early in the morning, 3am, set up camp, and then hunt. There had been a little trouble with a game warden, who had come out on a report they'd shot more deer than the law allowed.[21] But nothing came of that. Ma had a propensity for cards and jigsaw puzzles and went to a nearby church every Sunday. Fred missed his girlfriend Paula Harmon. The group was falling into an easy rhythm of leisure and if they didn't think too hard, they could imagine a world where they weren't fugitives from justice. It was a parody of normalcy.

Harry Campbell nearly blew the entire thing. While driving drunk on the backroads outside of Bronson (NE of the lake house), Campbell failed to see a Model T run a stop sign. The collision killed the other people, a young couple with a baby from Jacksonville (the baby survived). Campbell sobered up in the county jail. If the sheriff had received FBI flyers or participated in its fingerprint program, Campbell would have never made it out of jail. But this was rural Florida in the 1930s. The accident was reviewed and it was determined the other driver was in the wrong for running the stop sign. Campbell was exonerated. According to Karpis, Campbell also talked his way out by buying a new Ford from the local dealer and donating $250 toward the care of the baby.[22]

On December 6th, Fred Barker received a telegram from Joe Adams requesting he come to Miami. He drove down and arrived the next morning at the El Comodoro Hotel. He couldn't believe his eyes - standing in front of him was a suntanned Alvin Karpis. His friend had been hiding out in Cuba. Barker told him about the place they were renting on Lake Weir, the fishing and hunting they'd done. Ma wanted Karpis and Dolores to come up and visit.

Karpis was suspicious. He'd heard Campbell was there with Wynona Burdette, who had just been in federal custody for questioning.

"How the hell did she get away from the FBI?" Karpis asked.

"It's kind of a long story," Barker said.

Barker talked about a job in Cleveland robbing an armored car, but Karpis was not receptive. He promised to visit the Barkers soon.[23]

When Fred Barker arrived back in Oklawaha, he had a large bag of pecans and 22 boxes of candy as presents for Ma.[24]

They were getting bored and restless. The next week, Fred and Ma drove back down to Miami to visit Karpis. They went deep-sea fishing and after much convincing, Karpis agreed to the Cleveland job. They drove up to Cleveland, met Doc who had driven over from Chicago, and scouted out the job. Rumors were the city was still hot and the FBI was tracking down leads on them. Karpis, Fred, and Harry drove back to Florida. Karpis seemed impressed by it. "It was a gorgeous layout. The cottage sat fifty yards from the lake and it came with a boathouse and a launch. A stone fence, about waist-high, surrounded the property and the grounds were crowded with grapefruit, orange, and lemon trees. It was a small paradise," he would later write.[1] None of them realized one glaring weakness. Though off the main highway, the house wasn't that far from the road. As Fred showed Karpis around the yard, automobiles drove past in full sight. A G-man could plug them right from the window of a Hudson and never stop the car.

Karpis spent a few days with them, fishing and relaxing. Ma gave Karpis a Christmas present for the baby who was expected shortly and Karpis left.[25]

Bankers Building, Chicago IL

Early in his new assignment, E.J. Connelley believed that Alvin Karpis and the Barkers were in Chicago. What the "good indications" were that led him to this erroneous conclusion were not known. They had the Commonwealth Hotel covered where Slim Gray (Russell Gibson) was believed to be hiding with two women. Agents tapped the telephones to eavesdrop on incoming and outgoing calls, trying to confirm the presence of Barker and Karpis. But a night clerk at the hotel let it slip that the phones were tapped. Connelley didn't think it would hurt their operation, but he told Hoover that "after things have been arranged, the clerk responsible for the tip would be taken into the office and given a talking to."[26]

Their best lead centered on one of the women attached to the Barker gang, Mildred Kuhlman. The 24-year-old Ohio native had dated Doc Barker and then married him in the summer of 1934. She represented the flapper – bobbed and marceled hair, had already been divorced once, and was very outspoken (one of her catchphrases was describing things as "especially good"). On December 14th, the FBI received a tip that one of Kuhlman's friends called her in Chicago. Kuhlman invited her friend to come visit her at the Hotel Morrison in Chicago. She was registered in room 3121 as Patricia Lonquart.

Connelley asked Detroit SAC Bill Larson where the tip

21

originated. Kuhlman had bragged to her friend of the glamorous life she was leading with the gang, how they said they wouldn't be taken alive and were better armed than the government. Doc had even purchased her a $600 brown Manchurian fur coat. Connelley and agents Sam McKee and Jim Metcalfe went to the hotel and asked to see if either woman was registered there. There wasn't. When he asked who was in room 3121, the clerk said it was a Mrs. A.R. Esser. The phone records indicated all of Mrs. Esser's phone calls went to Toledo.

Agents kept the hotel lobby under surveillance. After 7 p.m. Connelley saw two women approach the front desk and ask to check out. They returned 30 minutes later with a bellhop and their luggage. But most surprising was a short man that accompanied them. Connelley had no idea who he was. The three went outside into a waiting Ford coupe. Connelley assigned an agent to tail them. The agent followed the car as it stopped at one apartment building after the next. It appeared they were confused and didn't know where to go. The agent made a crucial mistake and lost the car as traffic prevented him from following.

Connelley hated mistakes and was upset with agent Ray Suran. They followed every other lead available – with the plates of the car now known, they found a dealer who had sold the car to a man that resembled Russell Gibson. And the phone records at the Hotel Morrison showed frequent calls to a room at the hotel Commonwealth, occupied by a Mr. John Borcia.

Agents tapped the phone line and traced a call to a North Side apartment. While watching this building a few days later, agents identified Mildred Kuhlman walk past them on her way back from Christmas shopping. Excited, they followed her to the Surf Lane Apartments, a luxury building off Lake Shore drive. On the list of apartment owners, they found nothing obvious like Kuhlman or Barker. Instead, they saw "A.R. Esser" occupied Apartment 1. It was the same alias Mildred Kuhlman had used at the Morrison.

Agents interviewed the apartment manager. The Essers had rented the apartment two weeks before and Mr. Esser was away on business. All of the pieces lined up. Connelley felt he was close to breaking the case. He rented an apartment at the Surf Lane from which to conduct round the clock surveillance on Kuhlman.

On Christmas Eve 1934, Connelley requested authority to tap the telephones at the house of a Chicago friend of Mildred Kuhlman. By the 26th, they believed Doc Barker, Karpis, Volney Davis, and Russell Gibson were in or near Chicago. It seemed they would convene at the Surf Lane apartments. Connelley began to prepare a raid. He asked for nine agents on assignment in San Francisco to return at once to Chicago. Specifically, Connelly wanted agents Muzzey, Campbell,

Hurt, and McRae due to their familiarity with the informants and subjects in the case (Campbell and Hurt were also some of the best shots in the Bureau, a fact that did not escape Connelley).

Meanwhile, agents tailed Mildred Kuhlman. There was no sign of Doc Barker, but one visitor left and returned to an apartment building at 3912 Pine Grove Avenue. Connelley widened the net and rented an apartment there. He wanted no stone unturned. When the Barker-Karpis gang returned to Chicago, he wanted to know immediately and act swiftly.

Willie Woodbury was completing his daily chores on New Years Day 1935 when two men arrived at the house in a 1935 black Ford V-6 coupe. No one was home, so Woodbury greeted them and took their things, showing them into the house. It was Doc Barker and Russell Gibson. Ma Barker and Wynona Burdette came home shortly after (the pair had raised some eyebrows in Ocala at the stores with how freely they spent their money). When Fred and Harry Campbell returned to the house, the gang was reunited. Doc was still worked up about robbing the bank in Cleveland and he wanted to get Fred and Alvin to come back up with him.

The three men drove down to Miami and visited Karpis at his rented house.

"What the hell are they doing down here?" Karpis asked Fred.

Doc was insistent on pulling the job and needed help. Karpis took the gifts Ma Barker had sent for the baby (which still was not born) and sent them away. A few days later, though, he changed his mind and drove up to Lake Weir. Discouraged that no one else was interested in the job, Doc was preparing to drive back to Chicago with Gibson. Karpis thought Doc was a dim-wit, so they discussed how the Cleveland job would be pulled off. Karpis appeared to be finally satisfied. Doc agreed to go up north and get things ready.

How will I remember how to find the lake house? Doc asked. Then he saw the Florida road map he'd used to drive down South. "Well hell, I know, I'll just circle it right here and I'll know this is the town you want me to send word to. I'll send it in a letter. Is that the way you want it?"

"Yeah," Fred said, "just send a letter down here. Say anything in it, that my brother's sick or anything, we'll know they want us in Cleveland."[27]

The gang said their goodbyes. Doc Barker and Slim Gray drove up to Macon, Georgia and met Monty Carter (alias Bryan Bolton) and Willie Harrison, who were also driving back from Miami. Doc didn't trust Monty Carter and wanted to keep an eye on him.

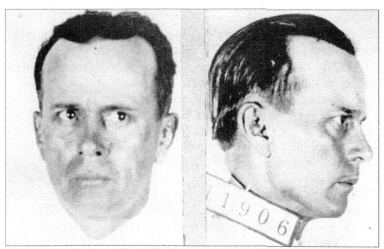

Arthur "Doc" Barker, courtesy FBI, 1922

At the start of the 1935, E.J. Connelley felt the increasing pressure to accomplish something. As he surveyed the state of affairs in Chicago, he had to admit an embarrassing fact. The Bureau had lost track of Alvin Karpis, Fred and Doc Barker, Harry Campbell, Volney Davis, and other members of the Barker-Karpis gang. Their surveillance on various people and places in Chicago had yet to produce anything. On December 29, 1934, an agent admitted to Hoover "there is no indication of the present whereabouts of any member of the gang."[28] The most visible public enemies had ostensibly vanished.

Connelley planned a crime conference for January 9th, in the hopes of creating new leads and reviving old ones. Special Agents from the Detroit, Kansas City, Oklahoma City, Omaha, St. Louis, St. Paul, Salt Lake City, and San Francisco offices were ordered to Chicago "for the purpose of discussing the case and its various ramifications with the view to bringing it to an early conclusion."[29]

On January 8th, he sat in the second floor apartment at 3920 Pine Grove Avenue and looked out the window. His agents had reported new activity at both this location and the Surf Lane apartments. The night before, Mr. Esser had returned to Chicago, to Mildred Kuhlman's apartment. They hadn't spotted the man yet to identify if, as Connelley suspected, it was Doc Barker. Two other men had returned to their girlfriends and were staying in the apartment just below where Connelley sat. Agents on surveillance duty thought one of the men was Russell Gibson, but they couldn't be absolutely sure until they could see him in daylight.

He had to balance patience with the need to not miss an

opportunity. Connelley knew they had a good location to raid. There was only one rear entrance to the building and across the alley was a fence where agents could hide. He planned a 1-2 raid. They would capture Gibson and the other three here first, then go to the Surf Lane apartments and capture Kuhlman and hopefully Doc Barker.

Given new purpose, the Chicago office agents' spirits lifted. Inside the Bankers Building, agents prepared for the raid, discussed the plan, checked their weapons. Connelley wanted zero mistakes. No Little Bohemia, no losing Mildred Kuhlman due to traffic. Then, the men left to take their places outside the two buildings. If any of the suspects attempted to leave, Connelley gave orders to arrest them.

Two of the agents Connelley specifically requested, sharpshooter Jerry Campbell and rookie Alexander Muzzey, sat in a car outside the Surf Lane apartment. It wasn't bitterly cold outside, but the men tried to stay warm and keep a line of sight on the building.

Then, Mildred Kuhlman and Doc Barker stepped out of the apartment and walked toward them on the sidewalk. Campbell slipped his Thompson machine gun under his coat and exited the car. Muzzey followed. The agents tailed Barker and Kuhlman about twenty feet behind them. Other agents that had been waiting outside the building were approaching in the distance.

"Are we gonna take them?" Muzzey whispered.

"Yeah," said Campbell.[30]

Barker kept glancing over his shoulder. Finally, he looked back again and Campbell seized the opportunity. He removed his machine gun and aimed it at Barker.

"Stick 'em up!" Muzzey said, pointing his pistol. "We're federal agents."

More agents rushed to surround the suspects, drawing their guns.

Barker started to raise his hands, but it was a feint. He turned and ducked between two parked cars on the street. As he put his foot on the icy pavement, he slipped and fell forward into the street.

Campbell and another agent were right behind him. They handcuffed Doc Barker and lifted him to his feet.

What's your name? one of the agents asked Barker.

"You know who I am."

As they brought him toward one of the waiting Bureau cars, the agents asked him where his gun was. Barker gave a quote that would become part of gangster legend: "Home and ain't that a hell of a place for it."

William "Bryan" Bolton

Connelley knew nothing about the results of the first raid. The surveillance at 3920 Pine Grove Avenue seemed to be a bust. There were no lights on in the apartment and no one had been spotted since 6:45pm. He and ten agents waited around the corner of a nearby building. Dread rose in his stomach that they had missed making the arrests – he assumed the worst that someone had tipped the suspects and they were gone. But then, around 11 p.m., a man went down the back alley and into the rear entrance. A light came on in the apartment. Shortly after, another man and two women used the front entrance.

Connelley walked to a Bureau car on the street and ordered the four agents inside to go to the back alley. That would make 14 agents waiting for anyone who came out the rear entrance. Then he positioned the remaining agents near the front entrance.

Connelley walked into the lobby with agent Sam McKee, Ralph Brown, and a third agent. This wasn't a luxury apartment with a desk attendant, bellhops, or doormen. The four men walked through the small lobby and pressed the button for Apartment One.

"Hello?" said a woman.

"Is Mr. Bolton in?" Connelley asked.

The woman hesitated. "No, he'll be back at the end of the week."

Connelley didn't waste any more time. He told her he was a special agent with the U.S. Department of Justice. "The building is completely surrounded. All of you come downstairs, one at a time, with your hands up, and no one will get hurt."

They waited but the woman didn't respond. Connelley pressed

the button again. "All persons occupying the apartment come down immediately or the place will be gassed."

There was still no response. Two minutes passed as they waited in the lobby.

Connelley pressed the button again. "All persons occupying the apartment come down immediately. Do no attempt to escape through the rear. The apartment building is completely surrounded and anyone attempting to escape will be killed."

Finally, a woman shouted down the stairs. "We're coming down!" Russell Gibson's wife came down the stairs, holding a dog in her arms, followed by another woman. Connelley ordered them both on the floor. Then he saw Bryan Bolton, sidekick to Shotgun George Ziegler, walk down the stairs with his hands in the air. Connelley made them all lie down.

What's your name? he asked the first woman with the dog.

"Clara Gibson."

"Are there any others in the apartment?"

"My husband."

Connelley didn't even have time to process the information. Gunshots fired at the back of the building.

Agents covering the rear of the building had watched as a man tried opening several windows to escape. Then the lights went out in the apartment and the agents scrambled to see anything in the darkness. A door opened and shut and footsteps were heard on the back stairs. When the man reached the bottom of the stairs, agent Doc White saw the man had a rifle.

"Stop!" White yelled.

The man shot and bullets struck the fence in front of the agents. Agents returned fire at the man. The man who had escape staggered toward the side of the building and was met by more agents coming around the corner. Agent John McLaughlin reached the man first and saw he was severely wounded. Bullets had hit him in the head and chest.

"Are you Alvin Karpis?' McLaughlin asked.

"No," the man said. "Russell Gibson."

Agents cleared the apartment. Gibson was rushed to the hospital, but his wounds were severe. Agents questioned Gibson about the Barker-Karpis gang as he lay there dying. "Tell you nothing," was the last thing Russell Gibson ever said.

When Connelley regrouped at the office, he expected to grill Bryan Bolton for information. But Melvin Purvis gave him even better news. The other raid was equally successful. Doc Barker was sitting in a room down the hall. Agents were searching his apartment as they spoke.

Connelley took a moment to process it. The case was about to break wide open.

After fingerprints confirmed Doc Barker's identity, agents began interrogating him for information on the whereabouts of the rest of the Barker-Karpis gang. Barker, reputed to be of low intellect, was still a big fish in the crime world and had been in and out of prison. He'd committed armed robberies, murders, and been part of the Hamm and Bremer kidnappings. He wasn't Fred Barker or Alvin Karpis, but it was still a huge success.

But Barker kept quiet.

Deputy Director Edward Tamm wrote that "the fellow is a tough one and is not going to talk."[31] They began searching the contents of his apartment. Other than the agents involved, no one else knew Doc Barker was in federal custody. Not even the press, and Hoover wanted to keep it that way. The strategy was to keep it a secret as long as possible, so that they might be able to draw in the other members of the gang.

For some reason Hoover thought "the Chicago office had a pre-conceived idea that Barker would not talk and accordingly would not attempt to secure a statement with the vigor which should be displayed."[32] The word vigor is used several times in different memos. The agents worked in shifts during the night to try and break him. One agent later admitted to breaking two telephone books over Barker's head.[33] The "vigorous physical efforts" weren't effective. Barker said nothing.

Time was of the essence. The agents were essentially holding Barker without any formal charges (Connelley was prepared to file for possession of an unregistered gun, a crime which carried a five year penalty.)[34] If someone had been expecting Barker and he never showed up, or if they had not heard from him in a few days, this would tip the gang that he'd been apprehended and all advantage would be lost. They had to act fast.

Word leaked to the press that Barker might be in custody. A reporter from the Chicago *American* called Ladd.

"What can you tell me about Doc Barker?"

Ladd said he did not know anything about him.

"Where are you holding Doc?"

We aren't holding him.

I want a copy of the identification order on Barker, the reporter said.[35]

Internally, the Division stopped using Barker's name in the office or over the telephone, instead calling him "#5."[36] Hoover believed that either the clerical employees or stenographers were giving the Chicago *American* inside information, or someone had placed a telephone tap on the lines at the Chicago office.[37] Pop Nathan felt the atmosphere in Chicago was antagonistic and the newspaper reporters were "'snooping."[38] Clearly, though, stalling was not a long-term tactic that would work.

On the 10th, the Chicago office held its crime conference, now imbued with an entirely new focus. SAC Newby argued in favor of re-indicting all of the Barker-Karpis gang for the Bremer kidnapping, in case any of them were killed (as a U.S. Attorney would later point out, you can't indict a dead man). But he was overruled. The other agents felt no good could come of this. If an indictment was secured, and an identification order issued, the resulting publicity would get in the way of actually arresting the gang members.[39]

While Barker kept his mouth shut, they turned their attention to Bryan Bolton (alias Monty Carter). He was implicated in the infamous St. Valentine's Day Massacre and the Bremer kidnapping. Unlike Doc Barker, Bolton was ready to talk. He wanted to cut a deal with the government in exchange for information he had about the Bremer kidnapping and the whereabouts of the rest of the Barker-Karpis gang. The Division had to tread lightly. Tamm warned that "we should be careful in making inducements to him... in questioning him, we [should] not show how little we know about the facts in the case."[40]

Then, under interrogation by Connelley and SAs John Madala and Ralph Brown (whom Bolton had "taken a particular liking to"), Bolton spilled his guts. He gave the location of the hideout outside Chicago where Bremer had been held captive. Connelley wanted more - he wanted Alvin Karpis, Fred Barker, and Harry Campbell. Bolton claimed to know where they were: in a lake house in Florida.

Lake house hideouts were part of the Barker-Karpis gang's modus operandi when they wanted to escape attention. They had rented a lake house north of St. Paul, Minnesota in 1932.[41]

Connelley wanted to know *where* in Florida.

Bolton told the following story: he'd left Chicago on December 19 with Willie Harrison, whom Bolton believed had been sent by Doc Barker to keep an eye on him as "the members of the gang do not trust him implicitly as they do Harrison."[42] They had picked up Bolton's wife and children in St. Petersburg and then drove to Miami. Bolton stayed at the Dorn Hotel, while Harrison went to the El Comodoro Hotel. The manager there, Joe Adams, was the gang's Florida contact. Bolton and Harrison left Miami in early January and drove north on Highway 41 to Lake City, Florida where they stopped for the night. The next day they made it up to 30-50 miles south of Macon, Georgia, where they stopped at Lloyd's Pecan Ranch. Bolton was surprised, when at 8pm, Slim Gray and Doc Barker arrived unannounced in a car that "was not dusty or dirty".[43]   Bolton ascertained through their conversation that the rest of the gang was located on:

> "...a large fresh water inland lake, somewhere near Jacksonville, Florida... the lake was considerably remote from any town; that it was in a section of Florida where good deer hunting can be found as they stated they killed three deer and that they brought back to Chicago with them a considerable portion of deer carcass...they also brought back fresh water fish which they had caught... they appeared very much interested in an old alligator in this lake known throughout that community as "Big Joe"; that the boys had attempted to catch this alligator and had placed a small pig in a barrel for bait, but that "Big Joe" got the bait and did not get caught... the boys had a motor boat on this lake [and] lived in either one or two houses... the lake was not far distant from Highway 41...   Alvin Karpis, Harry Campbell, and Fred Barker are at this lake...   Freddie Barker has a small Buick coupe with him and that the car is not hot... this lake can be located by driving from six to eight hours south of Highway 41 from Macon...[44]

Connelley didn't know at the time if Bolton was telling the truth or just talking to try and get back on the street. The part about the alligator sounded like a tall tale.

It took three days for the agents to realize that two state road maps of Florida retrieved from Doc Barker's apartment were important clues. In hindsight, even, it seems impossible that it would have been overlooked for so long. Marked on one map in the center of the state was the city of Ocala; on the second, like a bull's-eye, was a penciled-in circle circumscribing a chain of lakes southeast of Ocala.[45]

Just as Bolton had described. The details lined up.

Connelley stared at the maps. Lake Charles. Lake Bryant. Halfmoon Lake. Smith Lake. Bowers Lake. Lake Weir. Pecan Lake. Silver Lake. The entire area was dotted with little bodies of water less than 1000 feet across. The largest of them was Lake Weir. Dozens of roads led to homes that ringed the shorelines. It could be any one of them. But there was no time for waiting. He had enough information to act and anything else could be learned in the field.

Before he'd been picked up off the street, Doc Barker had mailed a letter to his brother in Florida. He'd been in Cleveland and made all the necessary arrangements. The robbery was all set.

The letter reached the Barkers. Handwritten in pencil, it showed Doc's poor education and gives a glimpse of how he spoke:

"Hello ever one how is that old sunshine down there fine I hope. Boy it is not so hot up here, for we are haveing some winter. I Bet you and Buff are not catching no fish now for I think I caught then all when I was down there. I took care of that Buisness for you Boys it was done Just as good as if you had did it your self. I an Just like the standard oil always at your service ha ha. tell, Bo, you know the Boy with the rosey cheek that Moxey is up here looking for hin and if it is alright to send hin down. I have not seen chuck yet I have Been Busy on that other he was perrty hard to locate. But will see hin right away, and see if he wants come down there. tell mother that deer was mighty fine and I said hello and her and the sqaw had Better not let you Bums Beat then in catching fish ha ha well I will close for this tine as ever your Big Bud
        B.L. Barnes [*sic*]"[46]

After Doc had left for Chicago, Karpis and Campbell decided to head back to Miami together, awaiting word from Fred that Doc was ready. Wynona kept Dolores company while Campbell and Karpis fished the Gulf Stream. The morning Harry and Wynona were due to head back to the lake house, he changed his mind and said he wanted one more day of fishing. So they stayed in Miami.

Fred and Ma waited alone in Oklawaha.

PART II – THE KINGDOM OF THE SUN

Marion Hotel, Ocala Florida

Connelley called Tamm around 6:15pm on January 11th. He wanted to take men from the Chicago office flying squad and set up a base of operation near the location on the road map. Tamm thought they should establish themselves in Atlanta or Birmingham. From there, they could rent automobiles (for anonymity reasons, not "the Division Hudsons; it would be better to use Fords or small cars of that nature.")[47]

Connelley and SAs Ralph Brown, Jerry Campbell, and Bob Jones left Chicago on Saturday, January 12th on a 1pm charter plane to Jacksonville. The three men had been part of the Dillinger Squad and knew how to run an investigation. Connelley planned to make Jacksonville a headquarters as it was "the largest city near to the point in question."[48] There was also a Bureau office there, headed by SAC Rudy Alt. They took three rifles and a machine gun. When learning of the weapons the agents carried, Tamm said "our Thompson machine guns were not much good against a bulletproof vest" which they knew the Barker gang possessed. But Connelley was confident in his three Springfield rifles, in his flying squad marksman, that the Jacksonville office had more weapons if needed, and shooting should be easy "as the ground in Florida is very level."

The flight touched down in Jacksonville at 7pm. Rail service was still more reliable than commercial air travel, so ten other agents (Wolfe, McDade, McKee, McLaughlin, Madala, Ryan, Sullivan, Melvin,

White, Muzzey) took an overnight train from Chicago and would arrive in Jacksonville the next day, along with three machine guns, two rifles, two shot guns, a gas gun, three vests, two sets of cuffs, flash lights, and flood lights.[49] At the Federal Courthouse where the Jacksonville office was located, Connelley met with Alt, advised of his plans, and tried to obtain the name of an informant who knew Ocala and its surrounding lake area. Connelley then called headquarters and checked in with Tamm.

The next day, Sunday, January 13th, Connelley and the agents drove 100 miles to Ocala. They followed the wide St. John's River south, then headed inland west. The area outside Jacksonville was sparsely populated, forested with pine and live oak trees, and dotted randomly with lakes and swamps. They drove across the future Cross Florida Ship Canal, a project green-lighted by the Emergency Relief Appropriations Act.[50] They also passed through the hammocks and scrub ridges of the Ocala National Forest.

They arrived in Ocala later that morning. The city was the county seat for Marion County and sat 40 miles east of the Gulf of Mexico. The name originated from a Timucua Indian settlement called Ocali, or "Big Hammock." The area was known as "The Kingdom of the Sun" and grew many citrus crops, until the Great Freeze of 1894-95 made commercial citrus farming untenable. With the temperate weather and fertile soil, other farming drove the economy of Ocala and surrounding areas. The main north-south highway in Florida, #41, ran through the city, and the Atlantic Coast Line railroad had a line connecting the city to eastern markets. But the lakes and springs also drew tourists, including American presidents who visited nearby Silver Springs, one of the largest artesian spring formation in the world.

Connelley surveyed the area and set up a base of operations at the Marion Hotel, located in the Ocala National Bank building. It was an eight-story stucco box, capped at the roofline with red clay tiles. The exterior had little decoration, making it look like a cross between a drab Spanish castle and a prison. Built in 1927, the largest hotel in the area sat on the crest of a hill and jutted up conspicuously from the two story buildings around it. Two blocks away was the Courthouse and main square. On stationary letterhead the hotel boasted of "all modern conveniences, coffee shop, dining room, open all year."[51]

Connelley had used this procedure before in Indianapolis while searching the farm country for signs of John Dillinger. Set a central location at a hotel with access to telegrams and telephones, then fan out from there for daily investigation. He was a man of his methods.

Connelley and the agents secured rooms. Then he went back to the map. In the middle of the lakes was an old citrus town, Oklawaha,[52] further south on the main highway. Just from the looks and attention the G-men in their suits were receiving at the hotel, Connelley imagined Barker and his gang were also sticking out from the crowd. It should not be hard to find them, he thought. Midwest gangsters should be as out of place in Florida as snow.

The rest of the flying squad arrived from Chicago and were briefed on their plan of action. SAs Jerry Campbell and Bob Jones went to survey Lake Bryant, 20 miles east of Ocala. Campbell, 31 years old, had been a detective in Oklahoma City who had earned a reputation as a sharpshooter. Hoover hired him away from the police department to train federal agents on the use of firearms (the Division of Investigation had just recently obtained Congressional approval to carry weapons). Later in his career, Campbell was known for putting on a trick-shooting exhibition in San Francisco where federal agents shot machine guns, rifles, pistols, and shotguns between their legs and behind their backs. SA Bob Jones was another "cowboy" hired to beef up the Division's staff in 1934. He had been the chief of detectives in Dallas before joining the government men.[53]

Connelley and SA Ralph Brown, meanwhile, went to Lake Weir and Bowers Lake, about 10 miles southeast of Ocala. Brown grew up on a farm in Vermont and had worked under Melvin Purvis in the hunt for Dillinger. He was parked in a car outside the Biograph Theater, just feet away from the sidewalk where Dillinger was shot and killed. Brown and Connelley could have been twins, wearing their suits, ties, hats, and pencil thin mustaches.

While trying to stay inconspicuous and undercover, Connelley immediately found information on the Barkers hard to come by. "There are at the present time numerous tourists in this vicinity who are not familiar with the country and no definite information could be obtained to identify the locality where subjects were staying."[54] It would only be a matter of time before stories of men in suits, snooping around the area lakes, traveled to whatever lake the Barkers were on.

They needed help. Local help.

On Monday the 14th, the Jacksonville office came through with Connelley's request for a reliable contact: Milton Dunning, a former Deputy Sheriff and native who lived in Ocala. The agents met with him and provided him the sparse information they'd been given by Bolton.

The story about the alligator hit home. Dunning believed that the described 16-foot gator lived in Lake Wauburg, north on Highway 41. Connelley must have been ecstatic. They drove out to the lake and met with a friend of Dunning's who lived there.

Do you know of Old Joe? Connelley asked him.

Yes, the man said, there was an alligator in Lake Wauburg like that.

Was. The friend said that the gator had disappeared around 1925 and had not been seen since. And no, he'd seen nothing suspicious on the lake to indicate a gang of criminals was hiding out there.

Connelley persevered. Later that day they went north to Gainesville and made confidential inquiries about the gator and the gangsters. The efforts were "without success."[55] Every lake in that area had alligators, some named Big Joe, some Old Joe, all of them bigger than the next. The University of Florida had even adopted the ubiquitous reptile as its' school mascot in 1911.

Connelley went back to the map. It had to be Lake Weir. No other lakes were as large. Promotional materials attempting to lure tourists to the lake highlighted its sandy bottom and clean water, perfect for fishing, boating, and swimming. And though it may have been his eyes deceiving him, trying to make a connection where none existed, Lake Weir was in the center of the circle Doc or someone else had placed on the map.

Connelley sent an update to Hoover, who was anxiously waiting in Washington, D.C. for word of progress:

1935 JAN 14
JACKSONVILLE FLO

DIRECTOR
DIVISION OF INVESTIGATION US DEPARTMENT OF JUSTICE PENN AVE AT 9 NORTHWEST WASHN DC

BREKID[56] BY INFORMATION AS TO DESCRIPTION AND ELIMINATION OF OTHER LAKES BELIEVE WE HAVE SPOT LOCATED IT BEING LAKE SIX MILES LONG FOUR MILES WIDE WITH MANY HOUSES AND COTTAGES IN VICINITY EXPECT TO COVER FURTHER TOMORROW IN EFFORT LOCATE ACTUAL HOUSES
CONNELLEY[57]

Rear of Bradford house, 1935 (courtesy of FBI)

On Tuesday January 15th at 8 A.M., Milton Dunning went with SA Jones to Lake Weir and drove the road along the north shore from the Barnes boathouse to a fruit cannery two miles away. Palmettos carpeted the ground and Spanish moss draped from the arms of live oaks like silver strands of hair, making observation of the homes difficult. Jones decided the pair should to go back to Barnes boathouse and rent a motorboat, under the guise of a fishing trip, and survey the houses from the lake where they would have a better view. In chatting with the owner, Dunning and Jones learned that "some strange people had moved in the Bradford home" which was near the boathouse. Not wanting to tip their hand as to their true purpose, they could not find a way to ask more questions without raising suspicion.

With their boat and rented fishing tackle, they went out onto the lake and fished up and down the shore. They kept a careful eye on the homes between the boathouse and cannery, looking for any signs of their subjects. Some homes had docks and boathouses covering a private motorboat. The gang would also have expensive automobiles, like the coupe Doc Barker drove. Jones had looked at enough photographs of Fred Barker and Alvin Karpis to be able to spot them in public.

But there was nothing out of the ordinary at any house they saw.

Dunning was positive it was the Bradford house. It was nearing 1pm; they had been out on the lake for almost five hours. They motored back to shore. Barnes told Jones that while they were out on the lake, an agent named Brown had been there and left a request to have lunch with him in Ocala. SA Ralph Brown, who for some reason chose not to use an alias, had been with SAC Connelley that morning. They must have found something, possibly a break in the case. Jones and Dunning left Lake Weir and proceeded immediately to Ocala.[58]

SA John Madala was a popular man. Purvis's secretary described him as "my favorite, laughing, smiling, helpful, unprepossessing, unassuming, everyone loved Johnny Madala." He was an energetic Polish kid from the south side of Chicago who had been promoted to an agent from a clerical position.[59] He stayed in Ocala that Tuesday morning and first went to the Monroe Hospital. Alvin Karpis' wife, Dolores Delaney, was known to be several months pregnant. There was a chance that during their stay, they'd had to seek medical attention and perhaps even deliver the baby. Madala interviewed the superintendent and with two hospital aides, went through the few maternity cases they'd had in the past months. All of the patients were local and personally known by the hospital staff. He showed them photos of the Barker-Karpis gang and Dolores Delaney. None of them recognized the subjects.[60]

Next, Madala went to the Postmaster in Ocala. He wanted to know if any members of the Barker-Karpis gang were receiving mail there or had rented a post office box recently. After talking with the clerk responsible for the boxes and showing him a series of photographs, something connected. The clerk identified Harry Campbell as someone familiar to him. But upon further questioning, he could not attach the face to the name of a customer. The two men went through the names of those who had rented P.O. boxes in the last three months. Just like at the hospital, the clerk knew every renter during that three-month period. None of them were part of the gang.[61]

So much for sticking out.

While Dunning and Jones were fishing the lake and Madala was in Ocala, Connelley and Brown had driven into Oklawaha and met with Postmaster J.T. Greenlee. The small city of 300 people had charming little homes built after the Civil War, including one belonging to Confederate brigadier general Robert Bullock. Originally called Lake Ware after a Dr. Ware, the lake was connected to the entire east coast by the Atlantic Coast Line railroad, which ran up from Tampa to Jacksonville. Many northern businessmen built winter homes on the lake, like the editor of the Chicago Gazette, the US ambassador to France, and the Bradfords who owned a large furniture store in Nashville.

They showed the Postmaster pictures of Fred Barker, Ma

Barker, and Alvin Karpis. The postmaster couldn't identify any of them. The only place he could think of that was renting on Lake Weir was Carson Bradford's house, "quite a nice place," that had its own motorboat.

What are the renters' names? Connelley asked.

Summers and Blackburn.

A shock of recognition. He didn't need to check any wanted poster to remember what aliases Campbell and Barker used.

They received mail and a number of newspapers. Curiously, the newspapers were always "wrapped so that the paper enclosed could not be identified."[62]

The detail must have struck Connelley's trained investigative mind as odd. Why would someone wrap a newspaper? Because they didn't want it known what it was, or where it was from. Surely no one in Ocala or Oklawaha cared about reading the Chicago Tribune. But the Barkers would want to keep tabs on FBI and police activity there.

Postmaster Greenlee recommended they visit Frank Barber, who lived adjacent to the Bradford place. Barber was a former employee of the Leavenworth Penitentiary, he said, a trustworthy man. A harmonious note must have been struck in Connelley's mind - Machine Gun Kelly and Lloyd Barker, among others, had been incarcerated at Leavenworth. Barber, above others, would know if a family of gangsters had moved in to the Bradford house. Thinking ahead, Connelley gave an update to Hoover and requested authority:

JACKSONVILLE FLO
958A
JANUARY 15 1935

DIRECTOR
DIVISION OF INVESTIGATION UNITED STATES DEPARTMENT OF JUSTICE PENNSYLVANIA AVE AT NINTH ST NORTHWEST=

BREKID AUTHORITY REQUESTED PAY SIXTY DOLLARS INFORMANT GUIDE INQUIRY HERE HAVE LOCATED PARTY WHO KNOWS COUNTRY AND AM CHECKING LAKE STOP CIRCUMSTANCES INDICATE LAKE WEIR IS LOCATION STOP AM LOCATED TEMPORARILY MARION HOTEL OCALA WITH THREE AGENTS BALANCE AGENTS JACKSONVILLE COMMUNICATE WITH ME THROUGH ALT JACKSONVILLE=

CONNELLEY[63]

Along with former sheriff Dunning, Frank Barber was the local informant and breakthrough Connelley needed. Barber viewed the photographs and immediately identified Fred and Kate Barker as the Blackburns, and Harry Campbell as George Summers. Only, Barber told Connelley, Summers and his girlfriend had left two days ago on Sunday. Connelley's disappointment must have been clear. While he was driving around Ocala and Gainesville in a foolish quest for Old Joe the Alligator, Campbell and Wynona Burdette drove right out of the area. (Barber didn't know, and thus neither did Connelley, that Alvin Karpis had been there also).

Barber reassured him. From what he knew, the Summers were expected back that very night. Connelley questioned Barber and other details matched up. Blackburn drove a Buick coupe. Neighbors complained about the excessive gun fire the men used in hunting and shooting off their dock, the lights being on inside the house and garage at odd times of the night, the frequent visitors and absences. Somehow these men had connections to the dog tracks in Miami.

Connelley and Brown stared out the west windows of the Barber house to observe the neighboring property discreetly. A small dirt lane stood between them and the Bradford house. Another house, the Westberrys, stood closer to the shore of Lake Weir on Barber's side of the lane. A line of trees and hedge on the Bradford property occluded some of the view. Connelley stared through the dangling Spanish moss hanging from the irregular curves of live oak branches. He searched for any movement. The garage Barber mentioned sat between the two houses, but he had no vantage point to see what type of automobile was parked inside.

Then, from around the side of the house, he saw a man and older woman walking on the Bradford property. The short man had oiled-back hair on his head, shaved to the skin above his ears. The woman had long hair and was slightly obese. They looked to be in the middle of a conversation. His pulse must have quickened immediately. Connelley looked at Brown to confirm what he saw.

It was Fred and Kate Barker.[64]

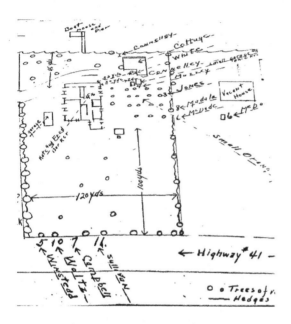

If Campbell and Burdette were coming back that night, along with who knew who else (possibly Karpis and Delaney), there was little time for deliberation. Connelley had to act. Fast.

He sent Brown to find Jones and Dunning and to recall them from the lake. A delay in the raid was unavoidable, they would have to spend some hours planning; but he could not allow the Barkers to be tipped off to their presence by two fake fisherman glaring at them from the lake.

Connelley began taking notes of the Bradford property. He sketched a diagram, showing the boathouse and pier on the lake, the guest cottage, a small garage for the cottage, and a chicken coop on the west side of the property.[65] The house itself stood about 45 yards from the lake and 100 yards from Highway 41, the main garage east of it. Connelley placed large and small circles on his diagram to indicate trees. He counted 18 small orange trees immediately west of the house. Squiggly lines indicated rows of hedges bordering the east and west property lines. Two private lanes would have to be blocked in case the Barker's attempted escape by automobile.

Connelley counted the agents he would have, assigning them numbers and putting them into the best positions surrounding the property. If Campbell and Burdette returned with Karpis and Delaney, that would put at least six people inside the house. He had 13 agents, and himself, on the outside. Plus the element of surprise.

43

That was it. It would not be another Little Bohemia. Not another false raid like he'd experienced with Dillinger at his father's home in Indianapolis. Like the success in Chicago only days before, he would capture his subjects. And if they resisted arrest, he was prepared to fight it out.

Back in Washington, Tamm received a call from SAC Alt around 12:15pm.[66] While never traveling to Oklawaha throughout the events, Rudy Alt served a pivotal role in Jacksonville getting information from Connelley and local sources, relaying it to Washington, and vice versa. In this instance, Alt had been in touch with Connelley, who advised he had found the hideout and was "all set for tonight." Alt would relay instructions to Connelley, but Connelley did not want to talk from the Marion Hotel and would call him later for direction. Perhaps he suspected a breach of confidentiality if someone at the Ocala phone exchange had been paid off by the gangsters to tip them on any suspicious activity.

Tamm did not want to relay instructions, however; he wanted to talk directly to Connelley. Despite the understated formality of his memo recapping his conversation with Alt, a sense of panic underlies the text. No doubt past failed raids weighed heavily on the deputy director's mind and he did not want the field agents making decisions without approval or input from the top Division ranks.

Connelley was instructed to go several miles away from the hotel and call Tamm. There were several small towns near Ocala, ten or fifteen miles away that he could go to and telephone from. But, Alt pointed out, "they would all go through the same pay station at Ocala."[67] Tamm was frustrated. They could not risk tipping off the criminals. He did not want to settle for giving the information to Alt, who would then have to relay the instructions to Connelley. In a raid, there was no room for confusion of orders.

Then, for some reason, Tamm had a change of heart. A few minutes later he called Alt back. If circumstances made it impossible for him to speak with Connelley, then "it would be all right for him to relay the instructions."[68]

Too late, Alt told him. Connelley had already left to telephone Tamm from a nearby town and would be calling him soon.

When the phone rang around 2:15pm, Tamm answered and first briefed Connelley on subject #5, Doc Barker. Due to media inquiries and pressure about whether they had him in custody, a fact that would tip Fred and Kate Barker and ruin the plans in Oklawaha, they were moving Doc to Detroit. But this was a temporary chess move, only delaying an attack they knew was impending. The press would figure it out soon enough. Much more hinged on Connelley now, to arrest the Barkers and search their Florida property for evidence that could beat a writ of habeas corpus.

Hoover was concerned about the raid in Florida. If Connelley went ahead with his plans, "there would be publicity, if there was any shooting, and we would, of course, have to take the people before the Commissioner then and we won't have the hide-out."[69] By "the people," he was speaking of Doc Barker and the Bensenville hideout from the Bremer kidnapping that they had yet to "officially" have sanction to search. Hoover wanted a plan that focused on the legal technicalities of apprehending the Barkers and helped both cases. The timing had to be right.

Connelley wanted to raid the house at six o'clock the next morning. He was convinced it was Fred and Kate Barker and by the morning Campbell and his girlfriend would be back. Connelley counter-proposed that the Chicago agents "take the hide-out at the same time the raid is conducted, which would be 5 o'clock their time."[70] There would be no way news could get down to Florida and ruin his raid. Evidence would be in place to justify both actions. Tamm warned that if the Barkers had to be arraigned right away, they would not have federal jurisdiction.

Connelley referred to his brief legal training. They *did* have jurisdiction, because they had an indictment from the Bremer case. Tamm fired back: that "will not hold water."[71] Probably just what he feared, he had a field agent ready to take local action without comprehending the full federal picture. Tamm told Connelley to await further instructions. The memorandum (which seemed to fly from one desk to the next in the Washington, D.C. office) was transcribed and routed to Director Hoover's desk. In a clear hand Hoover wrote at the bottom: "Do as Connelley suggests. J.E.H. 1/15/35." Then, back on Tamm's desk, the deputy director wrote: "Connelley so advised. 1/15/34 EAT."[72]

The next time Connelley made contact with Washington, at 4:15pm, "he was making arrangements to 'break' the case." He provided Tamm with details about the layout of the property, distances, how they would have to evacuate nearby occupants. The conversation ranged from disadvantages ("there was no natural protection whatever around the house") to advantages ("there was a motorboat located tied to a pier in front of the house and this angle could be nicely covered... they had plenty of equipment, including gas equipment.")[73]

Connelley was ready for battle, the raid planned in his mind from what he had observed first hand. But it appeared the idea was still sinking in at headquarters. Connelley wanted to talk to assistant-to-the-director Ladd about the people he wanted taken into custody. He was already thinking ahead to post-raid, to arrests and prosecution. Tamm wavered. "I advised Mr. Connelley that I would talk with you [Hoover] regarding the proposed raid and would call Mr. Connelley back."[74]

An hour later, Connelley had his answer. Hoover deferred to

Connelley's judgment in the situation. If he thought the Illinois and Florida raids should be conducted simultaneously, they would do it. Connelley had the green light. He proceeded to contact Ladd in Chicago to make arrangements for the morning.[75]

Connelley drove back to Ocala and decided they needed to be closer to the action than the Marion Hotel. He made arrangements for the agents to have rooms at the nearby Oklawaha Inn, a 1/4 mile east of the Bradford house. The two-story stucco building had a limited number of rooms. Agents parked automobiles behind the building, to avoid notice from anyone driving by on Highway 41.

At 1am January 16th, SA James "Doc" White left Jacksonville in a Division-owned car with SAs Grier Woltz, Daniel Sullivan, and Charles Winstead. They carried additional weapons and ammunition that Connelley had requested. The men were all part of the Dillinger Squad and accustomed to tracking down and bringing fugitive criminals to justice. Doc White was a former Texas Ranger whose brother was a Special Agent in Oklahoma City. He favored a bone handled Colt and hid a knife in his boot. He chewed tobacco, drank, and lived up to every part of his Cowboy reputation. At 56 years old, he was the oldest of all the flying squad members.[76]

White was good friends with Charles Winstead. Winstead was also a humble Texan and spoke with a thick drawl. The 39-year old with well-groomed hair, thick eyebrows, and large ears was a colorful character with an independent streak. He'd survived run-ins with gangsters before (Harvey Bailey, Bonnie and Clyde). Daniel Sullivan, "Sully," attended Georgetown Law School, had been at the exit of the Biograph Theater and rode with Dillinger's body to the morgue.[77] This was a serious group of lawmen and as they traveled through the darkness toward Lake Weir, they had one mission on their minds: capture the Barkers.

The agents met Connelley four miles north of Ocala and were briefed on the plans for the raid of the Bradford place on Lake Weir. Then they followed him to the Oklawaha Inn.

Plans were discussed, positions verified, weapons checked and double-checked. Now they just had to wait for daybreak.

PART III- THE RAID

5:30AM, January 16th.

The sun was not up yet. Waves lapped against the docks jutting into Lake Weir. The yards were dark, a slight chill in the Florida winter air. It had been a cold winter - a hard freeze occurred just a month before on December 12th and 13th. Connelley and 13 agents rolled their cars to a stop and killed the headlights and engines. They'd arrived at the Bradford house.

They could have walked down the highway from the Inn, but the cars carried their extra ammunition and would be needed to block the roads. As they disembarked from the cars and crossed the highway, they stayed low and made little noise, their quick exhalations rose as shapeless ghosts into the air. Connelley watched the house intently as they approached, looking for any sign of movement or escape. Only one car sat in the garage and he could see no others on the property. He had to assume Campbell had not returned overnight. It would just be Fred and Ma Barker.

They blocked off the private lanes with their vehicles and took up their assigned posts. SA John McLaughlin stood on the west side of Highway 41, to stop automobiles and divert them from the road if there was any shooting. McLaughlin, born and raised in New Hampshire, had earned a mark of bravery at Little Bohemia when he ran up to the door and lobbed a gas grenade inside.

SA T. G. Melvin took up the east side of the highway for the same purpose. He also must have noted the parallels between the two raids and his involvement at Little Bohemia and Chicago with many of these same men.

McLaughlin and Melvin were ordered to guard against the return of Alvin Karpis and Harry Campbell, who were reported to be in Miami, and expected to return to Oklawaha at any time. It was a dangerous assignment; any car that pulled up could have a tommy gun sticking out of it.

Four agents covered the north side of the house (Winstead, Woltz, Campbell, and Sullivan), to cover the exit from the house toward Highway 41. They were stationed 100 yards from the house, just off the highway in a copse of trees. Two agents (McKee, Brown) woke up Fred Barber and his wife, informed them of the raid, and offered to escort them to the highway for safety, but they refused.[78] McKee and Brown then took position behind the Barber home, covering the driveway where, if someone escaped from the Bradford garage in the automobile, they would enter the lane and make for Highway 41.

Five agents (White, Jones, Muzzey, Madala, and McDade) and Connelley crept past a vacant house on the west side of the property, crossed a lane, and then took cover behind the empty cottage and within the orange grove. Madala noted he "had an excellent view of the entire north side of the house and could very easily observe anyone leaving the premises from that side."[79] Tom McDade was a rookie agent who had been in a car chase with Baby Face Nelson shortly before SAC Cowley died in 1934. Here he was, in the heat of another major action. He had a direct line with the kitchen windows, thirty yards from the house, but noted "the only cover at this point was a small trench and some bushes which hid other windows of the house."[80]

Jones placed a piece of concrete walk, a 2' by 2' by 5" thick section, edgeways behind a small orange tree and lay behind it with his .50 government rifle perched on the lip.[81]

The nervous tension among the men must have been high. Experienced policemen, detectives, and agents that they were, no one knew what to expect or what was about to happen. They'd had little to no sleep the night before. Here they were, at a place many of them might retreat to for a week's vacation with their families. Instead, the most serious business lay in front of them. No doubt the death of SAC Cowley, whom many of the men had worked with, lay fresh in their mind. They knew who was inside, what weapons Fred Barker possessed, and what he was capable of. He was not a man to surrender or give in.

The sun rose. The lake water turned from inky black to cobalt flecked with orange. Connelley had waited long enough. It was light enough now to see anyone fleeing from the home. He stepped forward from cover. "In a rather stentorian voice,"[82] he "called to the occupants of the house, advising them that we were Federal officers, being Agents of the Division of Investigation, United States Department of Justice, and that they were to leave the house one at a time and provided they did so they would not be injured. Otherwise, if they did not immediately leave the house it would be necessary to gas the place to drive them out."[83] Connelley was probably less loquacious and formal in his actual words than in his report. SA Madala heard him say, "Come on out, Freddy, we are Department of Justice agents and have the house surrounded."[84]

Connelley waited fifteen minutes. SAs White and Muzzey repeated Connelley's instructions to the Barkers. They heard noises moving around inside the house ("as if someone were moving some heavy object,"),[85] but no answer to their call.

There must have been a moment of panic. Had they missed the Barkers? Had someone tipped them off and they had disappeared in the middle of the night? Connelley may have imagined in his mind the drastic consequences he'd face from Hoover if he'd let the Barkers escape right out from under him.

Ten minutes later, Connelley ordered Muzzey and McDade to fire tear gas projectiles into the house. McDade claimed one of his three shells went into the kitchen, though this is not corroborated in other agents' reports.[86] Muzzey (a rookie who had captured Doc Barker with Jerry Campbell only days before) fired three shells, but admitted because he was 50 feet away and the two windows he was trying to fire through were obstructed by trees, the shots struck the house to the left of the upstairs bedroom, one and a half feet below the window, and fell short.

A woman inside the house screamed. Then the house was quiet again.

The agents looked at the tear gas beginning to pour out over the ground, fifty yards away. There was little wind yet to disperse the gas. The last thing they needed was the sting in their eyes as they aimed their weapons or if they had to rush the house. More of the agents called out to the occupants, identifying themselves again as Federal agents.

Connelley decided to get more personal. Fred Barker and Kate Barker! Come out now with your hands in the air, the place is surrounded.

"What are you going to do?" a woman's voice finally said, as if she were talking to someone else in the house.[87]

Then, as if finishing the one-sided conversation, the same voice said: "All right, go ahead."

Connelley breathed a sigh of relief. The agents understood this to mean the Barkers were surrendering and coming out. So it wouldn't be settled the hard way after all.

"Come ahead," Connelley said to them, approaching the house from about thirty yards away with his 30.06 Springfield rifle leveled at the front door. "Freddie come out first."

Thompson sub-machine gunfire erupted from inside the upstairs southwest window, shattering glass and sending bullets into the sandy soil directly in front of Connelley, who fell to a prone position near the cottage.[88] 50 bullets were rapidly fired from the machine gun with its distinct rat-a-tat sound and muzzle flash. Then, from the first floor, a rifle shot blasted through the front door.[89]

Doc White hid behind an oak tree "twenty five steps from the door to the front of the house", near Connelley and the cottage. He turned and fired his .351 rifle into the house where the voice and shots had come from upstairs. This gave Connelley time to fall back into position and fire his rifle.

Resisting arrest. Firing on federal agents. Connelley's mind moved through the action effortlessly. They had full justification to go on the offensive.

Inside the house, the shots seemed to now concentrate on White, pinning him behind the tree. Then more shots came from downstairs on the west side of the house, splintering into the guest cottage walls. White concentrated his shots on the front door and windows, and upstairs on the south side of the house. Muzzey secured protection behind a tree, and fired three shots from a shotgun. Madala saw shots from the southwest corner and with his machine gun, directed his fire at that location. McDade, who was behind the hedge with Madala, also fired a machine gun.

Out on the road, Winstead, Campbell, Sullivan, and Woltz heard Connelley's order to come out and surrender, then waited patiently as they gassed the place. There was no sign of movement outside the house or garage. They could see McLaughlin and Melvin at equidistant points on the highway standing next to the Division cars blocking the road.

Then the gunfire erupted inside and outside the house. On cue, they fired into the windows at the rear of the house.[90] Though Connelley never explained his rationale for positioning the agents where he did, it is of interest to note that two of the flying squad's best shooters, Winstead and Campbell, were further removed from the action than the others. Winstead noted in his report that "the position assigned to the Agent... was on the highway where the rear of the house could be seen and the space between the house and garage covered in order to prevent Barker escaping from the house into the garage." Perhaps Connelley wanted his most accurate shooters there to cover the longer distance.

Whoever had the machine gun upstairs spread their fire further out, 300 yards out from the house. A staccato beat poured into and out of the house from the firearms, underscored by deep blasts and sharp cracks from the shotguns and rifles. Distinct flashes were seen from the side windows on the first and second floors, from the north upstairs window, the west first floor windows, and the east side of the home. The agents had no idea yet how many people were actually inside the house.

The bullets sailed far over their heads, causing splinters of tree limbs and leaves to flutter down to the ground. Connelley guessed that the fire might even be reaching McLaughlin out on the highway. He also realized he needed to relieve SA White, who was taking heavy fire. He ordered a short retreat behind a shed and moved into position in front of the southeast corner of the cottage. From this vantage, he could see the porch and upstairs window. He shot into the front of the house.[91] Machine gun fire moved away from White and thudded into the cottage walls in his direction.

Muzzey served as a messenger, conveying Connelley's orders to the other agents scattered around the house and carrying ammunition and arms from the automobiles parked on the road to agents on the firing lines. He estimated he made eight or nine trips from Connelley to other agents positioned around the house.

Connelley kept his eyes on the house. He noticed small details, like which screens had been shot out from the inside, indicating where a gunman might be. He also tried to understand what was happening inside the house. The Barker gang had the advantage. "They could see what they were shooting at. We could not."[92] The gunfire came less frequently, and when it did, the bursts of gunfire lasted less and less. He inferred they were trying to save their ammunition, a good sign for the agents. Connelley estimated that the agents had already fired 500 rounds, and probably 250 shots had come from inside.

On the east side of the house, bullets had sailed through the open space and entered the Westberry house. Mrs. Westberry had not heeded the evacuation notice and was home. As the bullets broke through the windows of the house, she secluded herself and her daughter in the bathroom. After a barrage of gunfire, she decided she'd had enough and was risking their lives by staying inside the house any longer. She dashed out the back door. SAs McKee and Brown, who had been covering the driveway from the Barber house, saw two people escape from the rear of the house.[93] Not knowing who it was, they advised they were federal agents and ordered them to stop. The two people kept running. McKee and Brown fired warning shots over their heads. It was hard to see them, since they were concealed somewhat by the trees and undergrowth. SA Brown thought it was a man and woman running along the beach. It appears neither agent gave chase and did not comment in their reports on the reason why. Whether Connelley knew about this potential grave error at the time it occurred is not known.

The sounds of the shooting woke the residents in Oklawaha.

The repeated shotgun blasts and machine gun fire was not your ordinary duck or deer hunting. Those already up for work (newspaper deliverymen, milkmen) began to spread the word about a "war" going on at the Bradford house. People began getting in their cars and driving toward the noise, and walking along the beach to get a better view. At 8:30 AM, Marion County Sheriff Thomas and a deputy drove up to McLaughlin's western roadblock on Highway 41. Word had gotten back to him in Ocala. There is no evidence to indicate that Connelley had included the sheriff in any of his plans, nor notified him of the time of the raid. The Sheriff and deputy took charge of the traffic control.[94]

For the next two hours, the battle fell into a pattern: an exchange of gunfire from inside the house, return fire from the agents outside, a lull where Connelley or someone else would call to Barker and whoever else was in the house that they were federal agents and if they were willing to surrender, they should come out one at a time with their hands up. Then the shooting would begin again.

Woltz reported seeing a flash and hearing bullets passing over his head and hitting close by. Whenever he saw an object at a window or saw a flash from inside his side of the house, he shot and emptied his 30.06 rifle clip of five bullets. He could not tell who was firing at him, a man or woman. Madala retreated his position about twenty feet and took a spot behind a fence post directly opposite the north side of the house. He counted 30 minutes that went by with no shots fired.

After this break in the shooting, Connelley ordered another round of tear gas projectiles fired into the home. The agents aimed the guns at the north side windows and fired. They missed.

They were now out of tear gas. Connelley ordered Muzzey to go to McLaughlin and the automobiles and get more projectiles.

After several minutes, Muzzey returned with the ammunition, and also with McLaughlin. The Ocala sheriff and deputy had relieved him of watching the highway. McLaughlin, Madala, and Muzzey took the tear gas guns and asked White, Jones, and Connelley to cover them while they fired the tear gas into the north side of the home. Madala crouched behind a tree. There was no cover closer to the house so the gas guns were slightly out of range for accurate firing. White got into position and fired a Thompson sub-machine gun at the upstairs and downstairs windows. Some shots were fired from inside the house at the agents during this time.[95] The cover fire gave McLaughlin, Madala, and Muzzey time to hold their shields and accurately fire the tear gas into the broken windows. Madala fired two gas projectiles at the house, both sailing through the broken window into the upstairs bedroom. Muzzey fired one canister inside. Like he had at Little

Bohemia, McLaughlin approached within ten or twelve feet of the house and successfully shot three of four gas projectiles inside.[96]

Then the agents retreated to cover and waited. Madala reported, "subsequent to this time no more shots appeared to come from within the house." Still, Madala and others fired intermittently into the second floor windows on the southwest corner room.

At around ten o'clock AM, Sheriff Thomas left the deputy at the roadblock and came down to the agents at the rear of the house. He carried a .351 automatic rifle. Winstead greeted him and because he was running short of ammunition, he asked the Sheriff if he had any additional ammunition. Only five shells, Thomas replied.[97]

The time in between bursts of gunfire inside the house grew longer and longer. The agents were trying now to conserve their ammunition and be more discriminate in their shots. Firepower concentrated solely on the room on the second floor's southwest corner. No other fire seemed to come from any other rooms.

A long time passed. No more gunfire came from within the house.

The Washington, D.C. office exploded with activity.

At 10:45am, Tamm spoke with Alt. A reporter with the Associated Press, a man named Wiles whom Alt knew and had a good relationship with, had called the Jacksonville office.

Do you know anything about a bunch of fifteen or so Agents down in Ocala?

Alt replied that he did not.

I just received a call from the hotel in Ocala and there has been a battle raging there since 7 o'clock this morning, the AP reporter said. The Agents are shooting into the house and the fire is being returned.[98]

There was no way to dance around it. Alt gave little information, but as a courtesy the reporter agreed to let Alt see the AP bulletin before it went out.

Alt assured Tamm that Connelley had 14 men and he "had loaded them up with extra ammunition last night."

Hoover read Tamm's memorandum and took immediate action. First, he called a contact at the Associated Press and told him the details of the gunfight. He could provide no comment beyond that, as no further details had been received.[99] At 10:54am, he called the Jacksonville office. Alt wasn't available, so the Director spoke with SA Lacour. Had Connelley made plans for telephonic contact during the course of the battle? Hoover no longer wanted to be out of the loop. He wanted to know everything. Lacour told him Ocala was 107 miles from Jacksonville, Oklawaha was another 13 miles from Ocala, and Lacour himself had driven through that area. He described it to Hoover as "not a thickly populated section." Lacour agreed it would take an hour by plane, then another 30 minutes to drive from Ocala to the lake house, "the scene of the battle" as Hoover referred to it. But there was no one else to send south - only Lacour and Alt were left in the Jacksonville office; all other agents were on-site.[100]

Alt must have returned to the office shortly after that and panicked to know the Director had called when he wasn't in. At 11:10am, he returned Hoover's call. He apologized for not being available - he had been at the Associated Press headquarters down the street. The AP bulletin would read: "A group of about fifteen federal agents and an undetermined number of men from Chicago were engaged in a gun battle at Oklawaha, about fifteen miles from Ocala; that the firing had been continuing since 7 o'clock that morning; that the gangsters are barricaded in a deserted house; that there are no casualties on either side, although machine gun fire was coming from both sides."[101]

Hoover must have been pleased. It was exactly the amount of detail he had provided. But he worried about his men. He dictated a series of memos that morning where he fretted about Connelley having sufficient ammunition and gas canisters. It seemed his worst fear was that Connelley had stirred up a hornet's nest of who knew how many gangsters in the house. The Barker-Karpis gang, Hoover wrote, were "the worst criminals in the entire country, and particularly not knowing the extent of their equipment and ammunition" he was concerned the agents would lose the battle. Alt tried to assuage his fears - he told him about the flying squad men he'd sent from Jacksonville early that morning with "plenty of equipment." This included shields, high-powered rifles, and .351 rifles.[102]

But, Alt had his own worries. He had not been able to contact anyone in Ocala to get information. For some unstated reason, he did not trust the Marion County sheriff in Ocala. The new Chief of Police in Ocala, however, had a good reputation and Alt got Hoover's approval to contact him.

Hoover did not want to take any chances. He ordered Alt or Lacour to charter a plane to Ocala at once. Hoover's archenemy, not on any public enemy list, was the press. Once Alt landed in Ocala, Hoover worried reporters would be swarming like bees to honey wanting to follow Alt to the house. Due to the remote location and the fact that the bulletin had yet to hit the newsreel, Alt said, they still had time. He'd send Lacour and would remain in Jacksonville to man the office single-handedly, to be available for future communications from Washington.

Hoover could not rest, however. As soon as he was done with Alt, he called SAC Hanson in Birmingham and told him about the battle going on. Hoover wanted more men sent down, in case the battle lasted toward nightfall. Hanson had six agents in Birmingham he could send by plane to Jacksonville. Hoover asked him "to take with him men who are properly qualified to handle such a situation, and to equip the agents with high-powered Monitor rifles...and machine guns and the inflammable type of bullets."[103] He wanted the Barker gang alive or at the very least, evidence of their plans not destroyed by fire. Once they landed in Jacksonville, Alt would meet them at the airport and provide further information. If the battle was over, there would be no need for them to continue on to Ocala.

Five minutes later, at 11:25am, Hoover called SAC Stapleton in Charlotte. Stapleton could only offer two agents. In addition to the instructions given to Birmingham, Hoover asked Charlotte to bring "flares for the purpose of lighting up the surrounding territory at night."[104] He expected this battle to drag out for many hours.

At 11:37am, Alt updated Hoover. Local authorities had blocked off the roads and were proceeding to Lake Weir to assist the federal agents. "Most of the firing was coming from the outside of the house, there being little from the inside." Lacour was leaving by plane for Jacksonville in fifteen minutes and carried with him another 1000 rounds of ammunition. Hoover told him reinforcements were on their way from Birmingham and Charlotte. Hoover wrote:

> Mr. Alt understood that nobody had been injured. I asked him
> to verify this, because of course this is my greatest concern.[105]

Tamm spoke with Alt a few minutes later. The Ocala Police Chief had heard "there had been no shooting from within but that the boys have been shooting from without and the place is completely barricaded and the Sheriff is out there with a couple deputies."[106]

It was a frantic morning of phone calls, memos, and second-hand information.

Back in Oklawaha, the house was silent. It had been over six hours since the agents had arrived in the early morning dark, and four and half hours since the gunfire started. In SA Jones opinion, "the occupants of the house were either dead or badly wounded." Connelley ordered a cease-fire and took the opportunity to check with all of the agents. None of them were hurt.

White heard noises coming from the small cottage southwest of the main house. He entered and searched the small house. In one of the rooms, he found Willie and Annie Bell Woodbury hiding. Remarkably, with all the bullets that had been shot at the cottage, they were unharmed. Agents had mistakenly assumed the cottage was unoccupied. Woodbury told White that the "Blackburns" were the only two people inside the house that morning.

White brought Woodbury out to Connelley and relayed the information. They showed Woodbury a picture of Harry Campbell and he identified the man as Mr. George Summers. Woodbury also recognized the photo of Alvin Karpis. But not too clearly. He thought Karpis had been there only once during the two months they'd been renting the house.

He clearly identified the Barkers as the Blackburns.

Connelley knew an opportunity when he saw one. Rumors from the gathering crowd had been that a man and woman were seen running from the direction of the house in an easterly direction along the beach[107] (Mrs. Westberry and daughter fleeing their house). They needed to know if anyone had fled the house. Connelley, McLaughlin, Madala, and Jones persuaded Woodbury to call out to Fred Barker and ask him to come outside unarmed if he were injured, so he could receive medical attention. If the lull in shooting were a trap - if the Barkers were lying quiet, waiting for the agents to enter the house before they opened up on them in ambush - sending the handyman in advance would ruin that plan.

Bravely, Woodbury agreed.

Woodbury slowly walked to the porch at the front of the house, no doubt expecting to be shot at any moment. The screen door was locked, latched from the inside. Tear gas poured out of the house and his eyes were beginning to water. He went back to Connelley.

One of the agents handed him a pocketknife and told him to go back and cut the screen to open the door. Woodbury went back a second time and cut the screen, pushed the door open, and opened the front door.[108]

By the front room, he found that Barker had moved a cot there and had been sleeping on it, the pillow on the end closest to the door, apparently to wake up if anyone knocked or tried to get in. Judging from the casings littering the ground, this was also the spot where Barker first fired his .33 caliber Winchester rifle.[109]

"It's okay, Ma, it's me!" Woodbury called out. "They're making me do this."[110]

There were no sounds inside the house.

Woodbury searched the first floor by himself, his eyes nervously taking in the kitchen, beer bottles on the dining room table, the empty living room and front and back porches. Bullet holes punctured the walls and ceilings and chunks of wood and glass and plaster littered the floors. The house he had worked so hard to take care of was in shambles. He came back to the stairs and saw blood on the treads. Tears filled his eyes. Woodbury stepped around the blood and climbed the stairs to the second floor. He searched all the bedrooms but one - the southwest corner where Fred Barker normally slept - then went to Ma Barker's room and "looked out the window and said he could find no one in the rooms."[111]

There was only one room left to search and its door was closed. Woodbury opened the door and entered the final bedroom.

Connelley waited outside, listening closely for voices or whispers.

Finally, Woodbury's voice broke the silence. "They are both up here."

Connelley couldn't see Woodbury through the broken window. "What are they doing?"

There could be a wide range of scenarios happening in that bedroom. The Barkers could be wounded, they could have a pistol to Woodbury's head, they could be giving him a shotgun to shoot at the agents. Connelley may have second-guessed his decision - did he just create a hostage situation? Had he sent a man to his certain death?

Woodbury's head appeared in the southwest second story window. Tears streamed down his face.

"They are both dead."[112]

PART IV - The Aftermath

Weapons found inside the house (courtesy of FBI)

Connelley and six agents raced into the house. White provided rearguard cover in case any shots would be fired from the house or someone tried to escape through an upstairs window. All of the windows on the first floor in all four directions of the house had been fired through with the Winchester rifle. When Connelley got upstairs, he went immediately to the bedroom on the southwest corner.

Kate and Fred Barker were there.

Fred Barker was lying in the middle of the room, face down, his forehead resting on his right arm as if he had lain down to take a nap. A machine gun and a 50 shot drum lay beyond his left hand. He was dressed in shirtsleeves and a pair of dark trousers and low black shoes.[113] Judging from the position he fell, he had been facing the front of the house, or the southwest window. Blood seeped from at least 10 bullet wounds in his left shoulder and chest, from either a .351 rifle or a 30-06 rifle. Two bullet wounds disfigured his head, one went through the back of his skull. Blood ran in streaks from his head, onto his arm and the floor.

Ma Barker was in the northeast corner of the same bedroom, lying on her left side, her bare feet drawn up toward her chest. Three bullet wounds blossomed on her chest, one right above her heart. A machine gun at her left hand held a 300 shot drum.[114] On the floor between them were machine gun drums, some full, partially used, and empty.

In the northwest bedroom, White and Sullivan found Ma Barker's house slippers on the floor underneath the window. A machine gun drum, which appeared to be fully loaded, lay on the table near the window. As White walked back to the hall, he saw a trail of blood leading from the bedroom into the southwest room where Kate Barker lay dead.[115]

When the press later inquired if the Barkers had any old wounds on their bodies, Hoover responded that "they were so badly shot at the time of their death that we did not check to see whether or not they had been previously wounded."[116]

Connelley knew his way around a crime scene. He issued instructions that nothing was to be touched or removed until the coroner arrived on the scene. From what he could see, Connelley tried to piece together the forensics. Fred probably reloaded the 50 shot drum at least once. He had moved from room to room, from the first floor to the second, changing his position and trying to throw them off as to his position and to make them guess how many people were in the house. He had been wounded on the first floor, evidenced by the trail of blood on the stairs, then come up here and received a fatal wound. Ma Barker had been wounded in the other bedroom and had come here where Fred was.

The anxiety Hoover and Connelley shared over news of the raid spreading fast was confirmed. During the long shootout, several hundred townspeople had collected near the north shore, newspapermen and photographers included. Sheriffs from the surrounding counties were waiting outside. The county attorney, district attorney, a prosecuting attorney, and L.B. Futch, a county judge who also acted as the coroner, arrived on the scene.[117] Woltz was stationed at the front door and did his best to keep newspapermen, curiosity seekers, and the public from entering the house.[118]

Coroner Futch quickly selected a six-person jury to view the bodies and held the inquiry. They made an obvious determination as to the cause of death: homicide. Futch then turned Fred Barker's body over and found a .45 blue steel automatic Colt pistol. It had jammed. A bullet had struck the butt end of it, splitting the handle and cutting a groove in the steel. It was loaded with a clip containing seven bullets, one that was still in the chamber. One of the agents' 30-06 rifles had struck the pistol, cutting away part of the steel butt and rendering it useless.[119]

Agents searched the bodies and house. In Kate Barker's bedroom, Muzzy found a purse with a zippered compartment. Inside it was a small brown envelope containing ten $1,000 bills and four $50 bills.[120] Later on the 17th, partially concealed under a mattress, they found a pocketbook and a $20 bill, a $10 bill, a $5 bill, four $1 bills, and silver in the amount of $3.58. Madala unbuckled Fred Barker's money belt and found in a zippered pocket containing four $1000 bills, $50 in his purse, and two ten dollar bills and three one dollar bills in the right hand pocket of his trousers. In total, Fred had $4,073 and Ma had $10,219.[121]

Already Connelley's mind was thinking ahead - these bills could be marked as those used in the Bremer ransom money. He ordered his agents to write down all of the banks, numbers, and series of the notes. Alvin Karpis was still out there, and these clues could lead to his arrest.

Funeral home workers from Sam Pyles Mortuary in Ocala were called in to remove the bodies. Madala accompanied the bodies back to the city. Once there, Pyles and Madala searched the clothing and Madala found a pocket watch in the front trouser pocket of Fred Barker. Pyles removed two diamond rings and a wedding band from Kate Barker's fingers and a diamond ring from the left hand of Fred Barker.[122] Madala took possession of the jewelry and later turned them over to SAC Stapleton, along with the money he'd recovered.

After Pyle cleaned the bodies, Madala took their fingerprints. He noted that Fred Barker's impressions "were considerably scarred." The Division had information that a Dr. Joseph Moran had performed this operation on Barker and others in the gang.[123] He forwarded the prints to Washington.

Agents used equipment from the Jacksonville office to take fingerprints around the house. The guns and spent shells were collected for analysis and to try and "bring out the obliterated numbers on same so we may trace them." They found two 1921 Thompson machine guns, two .45 caliber Colt automatic pistols, a .380 caliber Colt automatic pistol, a Browning 12 gauge automatic shotgun, a Remington 12 gauge pump shotgun, and a Winchester .33 caliber lever action rifle. In one wooden box, they would ship 142 pounds of "miscellaneous firearms" recovered at the house from Jacksonville to Washington, D.C.[124]

SAs White and Winstead went to the garage and examined the Buick Coupe parked there. It had a 1934 Illinois plate. They took down the mileage - 23,619. Inside the car they found a $40.76 repair receipt from United Motors Service in Kansas City, in the name of T.C. Blackburn. Two Standard Oil service receipts. A radio purchased for the car in Miami. White later found the keys to the car in Kate Barker's bedroom.

McDade and Whitten took photographs of latent fingerprints found on the right and left glass doors. The only place dark enough to load the cut film holders was in a closet of the house, which McDade said was done "under some difficulty, due to the presence of tear gas in the rooms."[125]   However, they put the exposed films in blue Postal Telegraph envelopes for forwarding.   By the time the films reached Chicago for development days later, sunlight had filtered through the envelopes and destroyed the films.   Connelley wrote to Stapleton in February expressing his displeasure: "It is not believed that this method of handling films is very successful, particularly in view of the fact that blue paper especially will conduct light.   The above is for your information in case future films are considered being handled in this manner."[126]

Mrs. Newberry, the neighbor who had run off in the middle of the gunfight, came forward and spoke to Connelley. She had seen the Barker's burying some bottles west of the house, in the orange grove. White and Winstead started digging holes in various places. The sandy soil moved easily, but they found nothing.

White may have thought it a wild goose chase, so he went to Mrs. Newberry directly. This time, she said she saw the Barkers dig a garbage pit not in the orange grove, but behind the house. Pressed for details, she said she saw them dispose bottles, empty cans, and other garbage into the pit and cover it up. White surveyed the grass and dirt behind the house. No freshly dug hole was found. Then, he discovered the old garbage pit. Digging through it, he did not find any money or anything of value. The Barkers were just trying to keep their trail as invisible as possible.[127]

It was 12:40pm. Connelley reported to headquarters by telephone. Kate and Fred Barker were killed. None of the agents were hurt. He gave Tamm a brief recap of the morning's events. Connelley had a tip on something at Miami, and a plane at Ocala was ready to send five men. As soon as things were cleaned up at the house, he wanted to go with them. Tamm suggested Hanson and his crew go from Jacksonville to Miami instead. While Connelley relayed details of how many shots had been fired at certain agents, he did not mention the sum total. He closed the conversation with: "It is not known who shot Fred and Kate Barker."[128]

Information about the shoot out was spreading across the country. Newspaper stories got many details wrong, including that there were three people in the house, that Connelley had knocked on the door first, that Fred Barker made one last desperate escape from the house before he was gunned down. The press called Hoover to see if local officers had participated in the raid, if Alvin Karpis had been killed, and if there were photographs available for publication. He did his best to keep the facts straight without revealing too much.[129] The coroner's jury adjourned for the day at 4:20pm.

In the lobby of the El Comodoro Hotel in Miami, Duke Randall sat with Joe Adams. The manager was in a bad mood.

"That's what you get for doing favors for people," Adams said.

What do you mean? Randall said.

"I rented that house at Lake Weir to that old lady and her son. They must have been wanted by the police because there was a terrible shooting match up there this morning."

Randall knew exactly who Adams was talking about. In early

December, he had run an errand for Adams in north Florida and had stopped at the house on Lake Weir on his way back. He picked oranges from the trees with the caretaker and then drove back to Miami. The Blackburns, as he knew them, were not home at the time. He pictured what the place must look like now that the gangsters and G-men shot it out.[130]

Alvin Karpis and Harry Campbell had been out fishing all day and returned to their rented home, where Winona Burdette and Dolores Delaney were. As their neared the home, however, Karpis saw his car parked a block from the house. Dolores and Wynona were sitting in the front seat. Karpis' intuition told him immediately something was wrong.

Dolores was so hysterical could barely speak. "You should have come home sooner."

"Take it easy," Karpis said. "Tell me what's the matter."

"The FBI shot up Freddie and Ma's place," Dolores said. Then she delivered the coup de grace: "Freddie's dead. Ma's dead."[2]

Campbell marveled at his dumb luck. Had they driven back last night, as originally planned...

Karpis and Campbell quickly packed and told the girls they would get in touch with them at the Danmore Hotel in Atlantic City. The men left the next morning on the 11am train.[131]

January 16th had been a long day. Connelley retreated to the Oklawaha Inn at 6pm and secured the telephone. He made sure his conversation would be private and not overhead by reporters. Then he called Washington and asked for Director Hoover.[132]

Connelley wanted to make it clear they had been fired on first, and only returned the fire. Fred and Kate Barker were confirmed dead. A machine gun was found in Ma Barker's hand at the time of her death.[133] He recounted the weapons, the money, the equipment found throughout the house.

What troubled Hoover were the reports emerging about Woodbury. Did Connelley realize how bad that looked for them, that they'd sent an unarmed black man into a house of gangsters? The reports were partially correct, Connelley later admitted. He only wanted to know if the occupants had been wounded or killed, and since Woodbury knew them he assumed the Barkers would trust him and not fire on him.[134]

What about the coroner's jury? Hoover asked.

I have to appear tomorrow at 11am, Connelley said. I'll limit my testimony to the fact of the deceased's identities, their connection with the Barker-Karpis gang and the Bremer kidnapping, and their past criminal record.

Do you expect trouble? Hoover asked.

The people and the officers down here are very cooperative, Connelly told him. Connelley knew Hoover analyzed the legal side of everything, and told him he had not contacted the US Attorney regarding if they were authorized to remove the money and guns from the house.

Connelley wanted to get Karpis and finish this business. There were enough agents now in the area, including those from Jacksonville, Charlotte, and Birmingham, that he wanted to leave and follow up on the strong leads in Miami. Hoover approved. After the coroner's inquest tomorrow, he was free to head south.

Hoover was adamant there was a leak in the Chicago office. The Chicago *American* had run a story that they had Doc Barker in custody. In light of everything that had happened, he would have to break the story. The safe house in Bensenville had been searched and photographed. He was ordering Doc Barker back from Detroit to Chicago and would seek indictments in St. Paul in the morning for the Bremer kidnapping.

Speaking of newspapers, Connelly said, reporters and Movietone men had been swarming the lake house. They had photos of the exterior of the house. But no one had taken pictures inside, and none of the agents had allowed their photographs to be taken.

Carson Bradford, the owner of the house, was reported to be coming to Oklawaha and would arrive that evening. Connelley was "going to tell him just exactly where he stood in this matter, that this man is a member of that crowd who runs the various race tracks, etc., in and around Miami, and it is possible that he is implicated."

Connelley took a moment to praise the county officers who had helped them. After it was over, they had congratulated the federal agents on their work. Hoover asked for a list of names of "men who were of particular assistance" and he would send them a personal note of thanks. Very slyly, Connelley told Hoover several of them deserved more than a letter, perhaps $50 or $100 payments for their services. Hoover would approve such payments for those who were deserving. Connelley agreed to call Hoover again in the morning and hung up.

The frayed ends of the rope were being brought back together. It was time to tie up the Barker investigation.

On the NBC radio network the night of the 16th, Lowell Thomas broadcast a report of the events:

"And now let's see where Oklawaha is. The lake country of Florida runs down the center of that glorious state, honeycombed with lakes and towns · a region of farms, truck farms where the Florida winter vegetables are grown. Oklawaha is on Lake Weir, a small town drowsing in the mellow warmth of the South. And now what happened. Fred Barker and several others of the Blackburn gang took possession of a handsome summer cottage on the banks of the lake. With them was Barker's mother, sixty-five years old. They call her "Ma." The Federal agents got a tip, so fifteen government men of J Edgar Hoover's staff helped by local police surrounded that cottage on Lake Weir· and the battle was on. The outlaws and "Ma" Kate barricaded themselves in the house and fought it out with machine guns. The Federal men with machine guns and tear gas bombs fought like soldiers on the outside from places of shelter, from cover. The gunfire was incessant. People from the surrounding country reported that the continuous shooting sounded like a small battle, and the fight lasted for five hours. The government agents riddled the cottage with bullets · and how did it end?

The announcement tonight is the chief outlaw, Fred Barker, shot and killed and his sixty-five year old mother, "Ma" Kate, shot dead · a machine gun at her side. The several others of the gang all accounted for, either killed or captured. It looks as if the Federal agents with one stroke down there in the lake country of Florida had wiped out the Blackburn gang."[135]

Hoover wrote a letter of thanks to Thomas: "You gave a very interesting description of the attempted capture which resulted in the death of Fred and Katherine Barker."[136] Clearly, he wanted to emphasize that this was no organized murder, but criminals resisting arrest. He also seemed to ignore the factual inaccuracies in the report (there were no local police involved in the majority of the raid; no other of the Barker-Karpis gang was killed or arrested). Always so quick to correct grammar and other errors in Division memos (the originals are full of X's, underlined words, and handwritten spelling corrections), he seemed to look the other way in this instance for a little national publicity of his men, overall favorable.

One man in Decorah, Iowa listening to the radio that evening took the time to write Hoover directly. "This is the first letter I have written to a public official, but I wish you to know that as an American citizen I truly appreciate your fight against the criminal element of this country...More power to you and your force!"[137]

Later that evening, SA McLaughlin was stationed on guard duty at the main gate to the Bradford place. Mrs. Newberry approached him. The shooting frightened her and her daughter. Her house had been shot into and she had not been notified of the raid. She and her daughter had to climb out the back window and attempt to escape while "bullets whizzed by her head." She heard someone holler stop, halt, and get back a number of times, but that she was so frightened she did not listen and instead crawled to the beach.

McLaughlin could sense a storm building and tried to head it off. He got Connelley and interviewed her further. She "left the impression that she felt she should receive some material assistance from the Government of a financial nature for the shock she had suffered in connection with the siege of the Bradford house." Connelley was clear in his report that the shots fired into the Westberry home came from Fred or Kate Barker from *inside* the Bradford house. Not from the agents.

The next day, McLaughlin went to the Newberry house to replace the windows and screens that were damaged ("only two") when Mr. Westberry stopped him and told him he would do the work himself. Provided the Government would pay him for it. McLaughlin gave him $10 and took a receipt for the damage done by two bullets breaking two panes of glass and ripping two screens.[138]

Connelley asked McLaughlin and Sullivan to interview Mrs. Barber, who lived 25 feet from the Newberry home. Mrs. Barber made a signed statement stating that the agents "acted at all times as gentleman." Mrs. Barber ended her statement with:

I am satisfied that the Agents stationed in back of my house did everything possible to protect the people in the vicinity of my house and at all times performed their duties for the best interest of the Government and its citizens.

The Barbers felt "Mrs. Westberry was absolutely too 'nosey' and untruthful in her accusation that the agents did not take proper precaution to safeguard the citizens of the community." Apparently after the shooting ended, Mrs. Westberry ran down the street and told onlookers gathered around the main highway that twenty men had been killed and her house was riddled with bullets, that shots went over her head and an agent had tried to kill her and her daughter by shooting at them when they tried to leave their house. Westberry had already asked the Barbers if they thought they could sue the government and collect damages, and where the Barbers stood on the position and what they would testify to.[139]

She was not the only one to come out of the woodwork seeking damages. As news and details of the raid spread, letters were sent to Washington. C.C. McCallon wrote to the Attorney General stating he had a judgment against Fred Barker for $1,200 for stolen goods. If the money wasn't marked, "maybe I could collect my judgment in some way as goodness knows I need it."[140]

No clue was too small to follow up on. A map of Kansas was found in the house, with some markings indicating a route from Ottawa, Kansas to Cherrydale, Kansas and some writing: "16/75W."[141] Connelley forwarded the map to the SAC in Kansas City. A deck of playing cards was sent to Washington to be examined for latent fingerprints.[142] They found a pair of ladies' optical glasses wrapped in a piece of cloth advertising the Jenkel-Davidson Optical Company, with offices in California. Connelley asked the San Francisco SAC to investigate who purchased the glasses.[143]

At 11pm, SAC Stapleton arrived from Charlotte with his two agents, Donaghue and Whitten. Since the action was over, their assistance was directed to keeping the area under surveillance and examining of the contents of the house. Stapleton led the collection of clothing and personal effects and sent them to Jacksonville. "The house, from the attic to the ground, and mattresses, as well as the entire premises, were carefully searched in an effort to locate any money which might be hidden, with negative results."[144]

Under a scarf on a table in the living room, Stapleton found Doc Barker's letter to his brother and mother, written from Chicago when he'd returned home after New Years.

Stapleton surveyed the damage done to the home. His report reads like an insurance adjuster surveying damage after a hurricane. He was not impressed with the quality of the home - in his report he frequently refers to window shades, curtains, and fixtures as of the "cheap variety." Stapleton detailed the hundreds of bullet holes in siding, screens, roof, windows, light fixtures, and more. "One bullet penetrated what appeared to be a family picture, breaking the glass."

In the upstairs bedroom where the Barkers' bodies were found, Stapleton counted 147 bullet holes in the walls and ceiling.

In total, he counted 641 bullet holes. Stapleton's recommendation to fix all of the damage: "It appears that all of the walls and ceilings will have to be replaced, as well as practically all of the windows, screens, shades, and curtains.[145]

Inside of house after the shootout (courtesy FBI)

The coroner's jury concluded by 12:15pm the next day. Connelley appeared as a government witness, identified the Barkers, and told why the Division of Investigation was seeking them. The jury concluded Fred Barker and Kate Barker "came to their death at the hands of Agents of the United States Department of Investigation in the protection of their own lives; while the said Fred Barker and Kate Barker were resisting arrest." Connelley secured a certified copy of the report and forwarded it to Washington.[146]

There was a problem, though. The guns, the money, and other personal effects taken from the Barkers had not been handled according to Florida law. The coroner was supposed to take possession of all personal effects and turn them in to the Clerk of the Court. If the coroner failed to do that, he could be subject to a suit from heirs.[147] Connelley wanted the US Attorney or an assistant to come down to Ocala immediately to prevent problems. The county judge was willing to turn the property over to Connelley. He wanted nothing to do with the legalities.

The coroner's jury had "commended the Division on the work it had done, in cleaning up the mob there" and he didn't want to lose this goodwill.

Was that in their official report? Tamm wanted to know.

They only personally advised me of their attitudes, Connelley said.[148]

They would send for the US Attorney at once.

Stapleton collected the money from Lacour and Muzzey. He recorded the serial numbers and turned the list over to McLaughlin, who brought it to Alt in Jacksonville for additional investigation. US Attorneys Page and House arrived in Ocala on the 17th and the situation with the money and automobile was presented to them. They suggested that the St. Paul office, the district of prosecution heading up the Bremer case, should prepare a subpoena duces tecum for the paper money and the Buick coupe.

On the 17th, the Marion County Sheriff received a telegram from Carthage, Missouri:

GEORGE BARKER WISHES TO CLAIM BODIES OF FRED AND MOTHER SLAIN IN YOUR COUNTY YESTERDAY STOP WISHES INFORMATION CONCERNING MONEY AND PERSONAL PROPERTY IN HIS POSSESSION STOP WIRE IMMEDIATELY OLL ROGERS SHERIFF JASPER COUNTY

Deputy Sheriff Williams answered the telegram, advising them the bodies were ready for him whenever he wished to claim them and that the inquiries as to the personal property found on these subjects should be made of the United States Attorney at Jacksonville.

The subpoena arrived and was served on Futch. Futch appeared confused at the order. Several memos passed back in forth in Washington. The purpose of the subpoena was to protect Futch, there was nothing he was required to do. The property, the money, and the automobile were turned over to the US Marshal. Somehow there was confusion. US Attorney Sullivan in St. Paul called the US Marshal in Florida and told him to serve a subpoena on coroner Futch to appear in district court in Minnesota and produce the automobile, the currency and notes.

Hoover was furious. The Division had received a letter from H.M. Hampton, an attorney in Ocala who had been hired to resolve the disposition of personal effects. At the bottom of the letter, he scrawled:

THIS IS JUST WHAT I THOUGHT WE HAVE NOW GOTTEN OURSELVES THOROUGHLY TANGLED UP IN THIS PROPERTY MATTER. GET OUT OF IT THE BEST WAY YOU CAN. I AM WASHING MY HANDS OF IT. I NEVER DID APPROVE THE ORIGINAL ACTION I MOST

76

CERTAINLY DEPLORED THE SENDING OF IT TO ST PAUL
JEH[149]

When the chain of custody further broke down in the following days, Tamm sent a memo to Hoover trying to explain where the clothing, money, and rings had gone. In response, Hoover wrote by hand: "This was bad action. We should have had nothing to do with this. Sec 29 of manual is still in force and effect.[150]

The memos and letters went back and forth - diamonds and money were sent to Jacksonville, Chicago, and St. Paul. The car was driven up to Savannah Georgia "to get it out of Florida," then returned. No one seemed to know the proper procedure. Hoover's final words, underlined, made his anger clear: "I want to get rid of this money. We have no right to be holding it. It should be turned over to U.S. Atty or U.S. Marshal."[151]

Perhaps he was doubly upset at his nemesis, the press. Collier's wanted to write a story about the battle and the lives of the Barkers. Hoover said "they were at liberty to write the story from whatever information they had at hand, but that the Division would, of course, not give out anything."[152]

Tamm directed Connelley to obtain photographs of the house, especially "with reference to the effects of the rifle fire, the machine guns".[153] Revels Studio in Ocala was hired and 24 photographs of the property, with notations, were taken around 10am on January 18th, then sent to Hoover on January 20th.[154] When some of these photographs appeared in public, Alt called Revels Studio and requested "that no more pictures be sold by her concern, made from plates which were exposed in the residence occupied by Kate and Fred Barker."[155] Apparently, Mrs. Carson Bradford had sent a telegram to the Division on the 22nd, stating she was assured the photos taken were for government use only. Alt assured her the Division did not authorize this sale.[156] When contacted directly, Mrs. Revels advised that the Bradfords had hired them to make additional photographs of the interior and exterior of the home and that these would be offered for sale.[157]

SAs McDade, Whitten, and Donaghue had a surprise as they ate dinner around 7pm at the Oklawaha Inn. Carson Bradford and his wife came in and took an adjoining table. As the agents were finishing their dinners, Mr. Bradford spoke to them.

"I see you are still here. You boys must like it down here."

McDade answered, "Yes, it would be a nice place for a vacation."

"When do you expect to leave?"

"Why, I don't know."

Later, Bradford and his wife got up from their table, finished with their dinner. As they walked past the agents, Mrs. Bradford said, "I hope you boys will stay over Sunday, otherwise we will have a lot of trouble with sight-seers running all over the place. Will anyone object if we string barbed wire from the fence across the beach and place signs forbidding trespassing on the property?"

Donaghue said, I don't suppose there's any objection to you protecting your property from trespassers in any way you think practicable.

While he had her talking, he asked Mrs. Bradford how they came to rent the property to Mr. Blackburn.

A friend of ours, Mr. Joe Adams, a former partner of Mr. Bradford in real estate and now the manager of the El Comodoro Hotel in Miami told us he could secure a tenant who had a lot of money. We had never rented it before but since Mr. Bradford lost money heavily in recent years we decided to do it.

The agents were pleased she was voluntarily giving them so much information.

Mrs. Bradford continued, We had no idea who these people were. When they rented the place they never rented the use of the motorboat. We didn't know the Blackburns were making use of the boat, nor the tenant house on the premises where their cook was living.

Donaghue was skeptical. He knew it was necessary, in order to use the boat, that they needed to secure the ignition keys from the caretaker who lived nearby. Lacour had also shared with all the agents the information from Watson's Garage about how Fred Barker brought the motor in for repair. How could they repair the boat if they didn't have permission to use it?[158]

SA Muzzey stayed at the Bradford house until the afternoon of Saturday, January 19th. He prevented reporters and photographers from entering the home, and assisted in searching the house and gathering up personal belongings of the Barkers. A two-page inventory of clothing was compiled, listing coats, boots, trousers, overalls, shoes, robes, dresses, underwear, gloves, shirts, and handkerchiefs. A silk kimono was listed, and some items noted where they were purchased (one light brown overcoat was from Frank Ray's in Miami). Hats were noted that were full of bullet holes. Also found was a 1934 Tennessee license plate 309 881 · the one Joe Adams had secured for them.[159]

SAs White and Winstead packed all the items in two wooden boxes and sent them to Jacksonville. Alt provided the list to Hoover and asked what to do with the articles. A week later, Hoover was perplexed. A bill of lading arrived in Washington, along with four leather bags and a metal suitcase. He sent the items care of Connelley in Chicago, pointing out the discrepancy between the wooden boxes said to contain these items and the leather bags and suitcase they actually arrived in. There was clearly a break in the chain of custody, a mistake. Hoover ordered all the property (except the automobile, money, jewelry, and guns) "be immediately returned to the Jacksonville office to be turned over to the local authorities for appropriate disposition under the probate laws of the State of Florida. This matter should receive the immediate attention of your office and the Jacksonville office." The last thing they needed was a lawsuit from an heir of the decedents.[160]

Connelley finally got his chance to interview Carson Bradford. Along with Melvin and Madala, they met him at the Marion Hotel. One can imagine the tense scene - on one side of the table was the man whose vacation home had harbored fugitive criminals, and on the other the federal agents who had shot the house to pieces. Whether Bradford knew it or not, Connelley had an anonymous letter Hoover forwarded, one signed by "A Miami Resident." In it, the man said "there is no question but what the El Comodoro Hotel at Miami is mixed up in this affair... the hotel is the headquarters for gamblers, gangsters, and crooks of all kinds an many deals are pulled off there. Adams, the so-called manager, is not a hotel man and Carson Bradford is mixed up in many shady deals."[161]

They started the interview with information about the house. Bradford said "Belle Air" was the summer home of his parents and he did not rent the place to the Barkers, he had rented it to Joe Adams, the manager of the El Comodoro Hotel in Miami. He explained how he knew Adams. Adams had married the past summer in 1934 and spent his honeymoon at the place. Bradford recounted the circumstances of the rental agreement. There was no lease or written contract. He insisted he did not know the Barkers and never saw them.

Connelley asked several questions about the Miami scene, the Biscayne Kennel Club, Bradford's arrest history (except for running away once as a 15 year old, he had none). "I have never owned or run gambling houses nor have I ever associated with gamblers," Bradford's later statement read.

Connelley asked him why he had rented the house under these conditions, never meeting the potential renters or knowing if they were able to pay the rent.

"The answer is, a man needs money, and I took a chance."

The Barkers made trips to Miami to complain against the people renting the small cottage, the Sextons. Adams advised him of this and Bradford requested the Sextons vacate. When they refused, he issued an eviction from the property. All of that was handled through Adams.

Connelley was not getting the answers he wanted. In his report he wrote, "This party is rather evasive in his answers and has insisted that he did not know any of the parties who were renting his place or what their business or connections were." In addition to not providing the answers Connelley wanted, he asked whether the government would pay for the damages to his house. As if to press the point, Bradford said "he might ask his Congressman to get through a special bill to reimburse him for his loss in this connection." Bradford claimed the house had $2,000 to $5,000 in damage.[162]

Connelley felt this was outrageous and in direct conflict with the damage done and noted by his agents. He concluded by writing: "[Bradford] is believed to be equally responsible with Joe Adams for the renting of this place to these subjects." But there was nothing concrete they could use against him.[163]

Something must have happened during the interview, the stress of the events and news, the considerable damage done to his house, the violent images now associated with an otherwise peaceful locale. Connelley said that Bradford "is of the crying type" and insisted on his innocence in all the transactions. In reply, Hoover hand wrote, "Keep after Bradford as I think he is just a rat."[164]

On February 2nd, Connelley received a letter from Mrs. Carson Bradford. She wrote to tell him she found several things in the house that did not belong to her (table cloths and napkins, a cooker, electric curlers). Two coconuts were found, one marked with "American Legion, Miami" and the second with "an ugly face carved in it." If Connelley did not wish to claim them, "I would love to keep them as souvenirs."

> After the first week when the crowds still continued to come & beg to be admitted I felt it rather selfish to be so sentimental over a house, so I opened the doors & let the first people set the price, which is 50 cents.

> Am so glad now that we are showing it & intend putting a big sign out front saying "Showing crime doesn't pay". Every one says it is a good lesson & shows the tremendous strength, power, & protection of our government. It was a blessing to all to be rid of such characters & I feel sure a government that stands for justice will do the right thing by us when they are absolutely sure we are innocent.

The letter adopts a very personal tone, as if Connelley and Mrs. Bradford had known each other for years (she adds a postscript: "Found the correct way to spell your name in the paper [she had addressed the letter to Mr. Conley]. Hope this reaches you.") It is part confessional, forthright disclosure, and thanks. Hoover, always looking for threads of conspiracy, sensed an undercurrent of insincerity in the letter. He wrote on Connelley's memo: "I am not so sure Bradford was innocent. His past associations are not very good. J.E.H."[165] But while Adams was later indicted, there was never any evidence against the Bradfords. He had tried to do Joe Adams a favor, and it wound up backfiring on him in the worst way. Guilt by association was not a prosecutable offense.

Later in February, Mrs. Bradford wrote to Hoover directly. She iterated their innocence and stressed the sentimental value of furniture in the home that had been damaged ("it seemed as tho [sic] these bullets went through our hearts."). Then she made a case that they, too, were victims like Edward Bremer: the Barkers never asked to rent the cottage Woodbury occupied; they were told they couldn't use the motorboat, they owed back rent, an electric bill was overdue. While she charged admission to show the house, it would take a few years to collect enough to pay for the damages, and they had to post a deputy so that people wouldn't vandalize the house for souvenirs.

When one sees how the government's bullets went through iron, steel, two by fours, walls, closets, and the entire house just riddled, it surely shows the tremendous power, strength and protection of our government and the utter weakness and folly of crime.

She then pleaded with Hoover to compensate them for their financial loss, stating they'd lost everything when the Bank of Bay Biscayne failed several years back. Hoover's response? "I regret sincerely to inform you that the Department has no appropriation available from which the claim for damages incurred in this case can be paid, with the consequent result that the only recourse that you would have would be a special relief bill enacted by Congress." He then ordered Alt to go and visit her in person.[166]

The governor of Florida, David Sholtz, telegrammed the Attorney General:

CONGRATULATIONS UPON THE SUCCESS OF YOUR MEN IN TRACKING DOWN THE BREMER KIDNAPPERS STOP WE APPRECIATE SUCH WORK BY THE DEPARTMENT OF JUSTICE WHICH IS IN LINE WITH OUR EFFORTS TO KEEP GANGSTERS AND OTHER VICIOUS CHARACTERS OUT OF FLORIDA.[167]

A.P. Buie, the state attorney of the fifth judicial circuit, had been one of the onlookers present in Oklawaha during the shootout. He wrote to Hoover:

After having an opportunity of observing a detail of your men, in charge of Mr. E.J. Connelley, in clearing out a nest of "Rats" at Ocklawaha, this County, I want to take this means of congratulating you upon your organization, it's efficiency and personel [sic]. The manner in which they planned and carried out the assignment was excellent, and has the 100 per cent approval of the people of the State of Florida. It was and is a pleasure to work with such men as Mr. Connelley and his associates. A splendid bunch of men, courteous in manner, and of the highest in efficiency."[168]

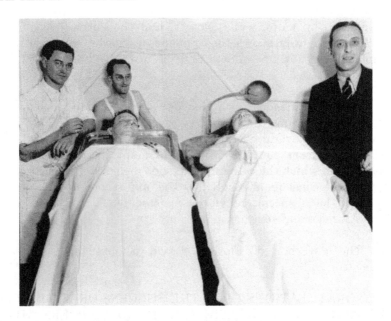

The bodies of Fred and Kate Barker remained unclaimed at Pyles Mortuary for eight months. After they had been embalmed, the public paid to view the bodies. Hundreds of people came daily, at first, and then as the novelty wore off, less and less. A photograph of the deceased criminals circulated, Fred and his mother close beside him, lying on the mortuary tables with white sheets draped over their bodies, their lifeless faces frozen with their eyes closed. Family attorneys visited Jacksonville and Ocala to settle the estate, where a local bank held the cash and jewelry estimated at $16,000. Once all Florida claims were paid, and the mortician was paid $3,000, a Joplin, Missouri funeral coach took them away to be buried in Oklahoma.□169 Fred's grave marker read: "Let us not forget He who gave us life, understands all the reasons." Ma Barker's grave read: "The darkest night shall end in bright day."

AFTERWORD

After I visited Ocklawaha in 2012, the Bradford family dusted off the Ma Barker legend and put the home up for sale for the first time in its history (a $1 million asking price). Sotheby's tried to spin the property with creative advertising: "Anyone interested in a hot real estate deal with a big bang factor?"

They created a special webpage with Ma Barker memorabilia galore. A catalog detailed the furniture in the house, which looked similar to what occupied the home in 1935. The home had been so well preserved, 80 years later, that bullet holes could still be seen in some of the walls and furniture. Links to FBI files and memos from the raid could be accessed for reading.

The listing made national news. The house had never before been listed for sale and the family had built another house on the property, so it hadn't been lived in much or updated. It was as if the house had been frozen in time.

But there were no takers. They tried to lure potential buyers by providing a map, showing options of how to use the land. One suggested moving the old house across the street to a plot of land. But it never sold.

The government tried to get involved. In 2015, the Florida Senate set aside $400,000 from the Land Acquisition Trust Fund to purchase the house. The amount was reduced during budget negotiations and the bill passed, but ultimately Governor Rick Scott exercised his veto.

Marion County looked to find another source of money to purchase the home (the asking price now $889,000). The plan remains to turn the home into a museum for law enforcement.

Meanwhile, other than the trees that have grown up around the house and the level of the lake dropping, the home looks similar to the day E.J. Connelley and his squad found it. If you close your eyes and imagine, the sounds of Hudson coupes and Tommy guns is not that far away.

Two notes of clarification – the current spelling is Ocklawaha; in 1935 it was Oklawaha. In January 1935, the FBI went by the moniker the Division of Investigation. It wasn't until later that year that it became the Federal Bureau of Investigation.

---

[1] EJC to Hoover, 7-576-3619

[2] Hoover to Tamm, memo, 7-576-3645

[3] Hoover to Tamm, memo, 7-576-3608x

[4] www.wikipedia.org/wiki/Barker_Gang

[5] Maccabee, Paul. John Dillinger slept here: a crooks' tour of crime and corruption in St. Paul, 1920-1936. St. Paul: Minnesota Historical Society Press, 1995. p 106

[6] Maccabee, Paul. John Dillinger slept here: a crooks' tour of crime and corruption in St. Paul, 1920-1936. St. Paul: Minnesota Historical Society Press, 1995. Book. p 102

[7] Burrough, Bryan. Public Enemies. New York: Penguin Press, 2004. Book. p 263

[8] SAC Stapleton would later dispute the cost, writing: "this is grossly exaggerated, unless this includes the cost of the land upon which it is located." Connelley report, February 5 1935, BKF#4315

[9] Statement of Carson Bradford, January 29 1935, BKF #4743

[10] BKF #4315; Bradford and Adams statements, BKF #4743

[11] Statement from William Milton Johnson, BKF #4743

[12] In a later statement, Adams denied sending newspapers, saying "I never did that because I didn't want to be bothered with mailing the papers to them each day." However, the evidence from Johnson, Willie Woodbury, the telegram, and the Oklawaha Post Office indicates otherwise.

[13] Report, BKF# 4315

[14] Special Agent J.C. White report, BKF# 4315

[15] Special Agent J.C.White report, BKF# 4315

[16] Report, BKF# 4315

[17] Report, BKF# 4315

[18] Statement from Saxton in Connelley report, BKF#4315; the report includes "it is the opinion of the writer that she [Mrs. Sexton] became very intimate with Harry Campbell and probably engaged in sexual relations with him."

[19] Special Agent J.C. White report, BKF #4315

[20] Special Agent D.P. Sullivan report, BKF #4315

[21] Statement of Wynona Burdette, January 21 1935, BKF#4296

[22] Tamm memo to Hoover, January 22 1935, BKF #3995

[23] Burrough, Bryan. Public Enemies. New York: Penguin Press, 2004. Book., page 494

[24] Special Agent D.P. Sullivan report, BKF#4315

[25] Burrough, Bryan. Public Enemies. New York: Penguin Press, 2004. Book., page 494; Report by Special Agent D.P. Sullivan, BKF #4315

[26] Hoover to Tamm, memo, 7-576-3608x

[27] Burrough, Bryan. Public Enemies. New York: Penguin Press, 2004. Book., page 495

[28] Newby memo to Hoover, December 29 1934, BKF 7-576

[29] Hoover to Tolson, January 5 1935, BKF #3709; Memorandum For the Director, January 12 1935, R.E. Newby; Memorandum For the Director, January 9 1935 9am, T.D. Quinn

[30] Bryan Burroughs Public Enemies

[31] Tamm memo to Hoover, January 8 1935, BKF #3765

[32] Tamm memo to Hoover, January 14 1935, BKF #3909

[33] Burrough, Bryan. Public Enemies. New York: Penguin Press, 2004. Book., page 500

[34] Tamm memo to Hoover, January 11 1935, BKF #3745

[35] Tamm memo to Hoover, January 15 1935, BKF #3770

[36] Tamm memo to Hoover, January 11 1935, BKF #3750

[37] Tamm memo to Hoover, January 17 1935, BKF #3873; Memorandum for the Director, February 8 1935, E.A. Tamm

[38] Tamm memo to Hoover, January 11 1935, BKF #3742

[39] Tolson memo to Hoover, January 16 1935, BKF #3822

[40] Tamm memo to Hoover, January 11 1935, BKF #3742

[41] Maccabee, Paul. John Dillinger slept here: a crooks' tour of crime and corruption in St. Paul, 1920-1936. St. Paul: Minnesota Historical Society Press, 1995. Book., page 115

[42] Memorandum for Special Agent in Charge E.J. Connelley, January 11 1935, R.D. Brown

[43] Ralph Brown memo to SAC Connelley, January 11 1935, BKF 3869

[44] Ralph Brown memo to SAC Connelley, January 11 1935, BKF 3869

[45] Tamm memo to Hoover, January 12 1935, BKF #3775; two maps as indicated in Memorandum for the Director, February 3 1935, 7-576-4648

[46] Connelley report, Bremer Kidnapping File (BKF), February 5, 1935, 7-576-4315, page 52; hereafter shortened to BKF #4315

[47] Tamm memo to Hoover, January 11 1935, BKF #3954

[48] Tamm memo to Hoover, January 12 1935, BKF #3775

[49] Tamm memo to Hoover, January 12th 1935, BKF #3775

[50] Using lakes, rivers, and newly dug canals, the Ship Canal would one day connect the Atlantic Ocean with the Gulf of Mexico. Or so proponents thought. The project, first proposed by Spain's King Philip II in 1567, was officially canceled in 1991. Remnants can still be seen today.

[51] BKF #4315

[52] The name Oklawaha, believed to be a corruption of the Creek Indian "ak-lowahe," meant "muddy."

[53]   www.historicalgmen.com/squarespace.com/agents-of-the-thirties-

biographies

[54] Connelley report, BKF#4315,

[55] Connelley report, BKF#4315

[56] Case name for the Bremer Kidnapping

[57] Postal telegram, January 15 1935, BKF #3791

[58] Special Agent R.L. Jones report, BKF #4315

[59] www.historicalgmen.squarespace.com/agents-of-the-thirties-biographie/

[60] Special Agent John L. Madala report, BKF #4315

[61] Special Agent John L. Madala report, BKF #4315

[62] SAC Connelley report, BKF #4315

[63] Postal telegram, January 15 1935, BKF #3780

[64] Tamm erroneously reported to Hoover that Connelley had also seen another man there, thought to be Karpis or Campbell, and at least two women (Tamm memo to Hoover, January 15 1935, BKF #3809). Connelley's own report contains no such details.

[65] Connelley's hand drawn diagram is available in the FBI archives, BKF #4315

[66] Tamm memo to Hoover, January 15 1935, BKF #3766

[67] Tamm memo to Hoover, January 15 1935, BKF #3766

[68] Tamm memo to Hoover, January 15 1935, BKF #3766

[69] Tamm memo to Hoover, January 15 1935, BKF #3809

[70] Tamm memo to Hoover, January 15 1935, BKF #3809

[71] Tamm memo to Hoover, January 15 1935, BKF #3809

[72] Tamm memo to Hoover, January 15 1935, BKF #3809

[73] Tamm memo to Hoover, January 15 1935, BKF #3705

[74] Tamm memo to Hoover, January 15 1935, BKF #3705

[75] Tamm memo to Hoover, January 15 1935, BKF #3701

[76] Burrough, Bryan. Public Enemies. New York: Penguin Press, 2004. Book.

[77] www.historicalgmen.squarespace.com/agents-of-the-thirties-biographie/

[78] Statement of Mrs.F.G. Barber, BKF #4315

[79] Madala report to Connelley, BKF #4315

[80] McDade memo to Connelley, BKF #4315

[81] Special Agent R. L. Jones report, BKF #4315

[82] Special Agent Alex A. Muzzey report, BKF #4315

[83] Connelley report, BKF #4315

[84] Madala memo to Connelley, BKF #4315

[85] Muzzey report, BKF #4315

[86] Woltz said they "seemed to bounce off" the house; White said "they failed to go into the house."

[87] Special Agent J.C.White report, BKF #4315

[88] Special Agent J.C. White report, BKF #4315; Several agents refer to

the room where the Barkers were later found, as the northwest. Stapleton's diagram inaccurately shows the house rotated 45 degrees on the compass and may be the basis for this confusion. Connelley's diagram is correct - the front of the house faces due south toward the lake, and the rear due north.

[89] Connelley report, BKF #4315

[90] C.B. Winstead report, BKF #4315

[91] Connelley report, BKF #4315

[92] Associated Press, August 4, 1954 "Earl Connelley, Noted for Kidnap Cases, Quits FBI"

[93] Sam McKee tried to question Pretty Boy Floyd minutes before his death, as recounted by Bryan Burrough, gave the infamous reply, "I ain't tellin' you nothin', you son of a bitch." Burrough, Bryan. Public Enemies. New York: Penguin Press, 2004. Book.

[94] Special Agent J.T. McLaughlin report, BKF #4315

[95] Special Agent J.C.White, BKF #4315

[96] White corroborated this fact in his report. The agents were very sensitive about any criticism they might receive regarding the accuracy of the gas guns. McLaughlin later wrote in his report: "It might be stated in connection with the gassing of this house considerable difficulty was experienced due to the fact that all windows bore full length screens, which were practically new, and further that it was almost impossible to approach the house within range distance of the gas guns."

[97] Special Agent C.B. Winstead report, BKF #4315

[98] Tamm memo to Hoover, January 16 1935, BKF #3822

[99] Hoover memo to Tamm, January 16 1935, BKF #3796

[100] Hoover memo to Tamm, January 16 1935, BKF #3819

[101] Hoover memo to Tamm, January 16 1935, BKF #3820

[102] Hoover memo to Tamm, January 16 1935, BKF #3820

[103] Hoover memo to Tamm, January 16 1935, BKF #3782

[104] Hoover memo to Tamm, January 16 1935,BKF #3783

[105] Hoover memo to Tamm, January 16 1935, BKF #3795

[106] Tamm memo to Hoover, January 16 1935, BKF #3813

[107] Madala report, BKF #4315

[108] Burrough, Bryan. Public Enemies. New York: Penguin Press, 2004. Book., page 507

[109] E.J. Connelley report, BKF #4315

[110] Burrough, Bryan. Public Enemies. New York: Penguin Press, 2004. Book. page 507

[111] Hoover memo to Tamm, January 31 1935, BKF #4281

[112] E. J. Connelley report, BKF #4315; Burrough, Bryan. Public Enemies. New York: Penguin Press, 2004. Book. page 507

[113] Special Agent J.C. White report, BKF #4315

[114] While it is disputed whether Ma Barker participated in the shooting, several agents included this in their reports. If it was fiction, then they colluded to include the detail before writing their separate reports. A later laboratory report dated February 6th 1935 said that "22 of these .45 calibre cartridge cases were fired from the Thompson sub-machine gun found lying near Ma Baker." Laboratory report, February 6 1935, BKF #4421.

[115] Special Agent J.C. White report, BKF #4315

[116] Hoover memo to Tamm, January 26, 1935 BKF #4089

[117] Connelley report, BKF #4315

[118] He would remain on guard duty through the night with White and Winstead.

[119] Special Agent J.C.White, BKF #4315

[120] This proved to be the source of an in-office feud; Whitten wrote that while at the breakfast table on the 17th, Muzzey approach he and Lacour and said "I thought you fellows said you found some money" and then proceeded to count out 10 $1,000 bills. "Where did you get that?" Whitten said. "Out of the pocketbook you told me you searched." Lacour admitted he saw the old brown envelope in a compartment in the pocketbook, but that it appeared to be empty and he did not open it. Rubbing salt in the wound, Muzzey added that four $50 bills where also found in a second zippered compartment.

[121] To put this into perspective, on agent Winstead's 1935 updated application, he listed as an acceptable *annual* salary $3800. www.historicalgmen.squarespace.com/storage/win35app.pdf

[122] Alt letter to St. Paul SAC, January 21 1935, BKF #4117

[123] Fred and Doc Barker murdered Moran in Toledo after he had been bragging about the fingerprint surgeries he'd performed for the gang. Burrough, Bryan. Public Enemies. New York: Penguin Press, 2004. Book., page 432

[124] Bill of Lading, Railway Express Agency, January 22 1935, BKF #3921

[125] McDade memo for SAC E. J. Connelley, February 23 1935, BKF #4842

[126] Connelley letter to SAC Stapleton, February 4 1935, BKF #4319

[127] Special Agent J.C. White report, BKF #4315

[128] Tamm memo to Hoover, January 16 1935, BKF #3772

[129] Hoover memorandum to Tamm, January 16 1935 BKF #3787; Hoover memo to Tamm, January 16 1935 BKF #3786; Hoover memo to Tamm, January 16th 1935 BKF #3784; Hoover memo to Tamm, January 16th 1935 BKF #3788; Tamm memorandum to Hoover, January 16th, BKF #3794

[130] Statement of Henry Randall, BKF#4743

[131] Statement of Winona Burdette, January 20 1935, BKF #3857 and

4296

[132] Hoover memo to Tamm, January 16 1935, BKF #3821.

[133] Hoover would be blamed for trying to make a case for killing Ma Barker, who had no outstanding warrants or crimes to her name. The detail is corroborated in several agents' reports. Clyde Tolson would admit in a January 16th memo that "it is true that Fred Barker was wanted for murder but there is no criminal record of Maw Barker."

[134] Hoover memo to Tamm, January 31, 1935 BKF #4281

[135] BKF #4324

[136] Hoover letter to Lowell Thomas, February 4 1935, BKF #4324

[137] William Sevatson letter to Hoover, January 16 1935, BKF #4020

[138] McLaughlin memo to SAC Connelley, BKF #4315

[139] Special Agent J.T. McLaughlin report, BKF #4315

[140] C.C. McCallon letter to Hon Homer S Cummings, January 18 1935, BKF#4075

[141] Connelley letter to Kansas City SAC, January 20 1935,BKF #7-576-X

[142] Connelley letter to Hoover, January 28 1935, BKF #4116

[143] Connelley letter to San Francisco SAC, January 24 1935, BKF #4049

[144] Special Agent in Charge T. N. Stapleton, BKF #4315

[145] SAC Stapleton memo to Connelley, BKF #4315

[146] Connelley report, BKF #4315, 4319

[147] Tamm memo to Hoover, January 16 1935, BKF #3872

[148] Tamm memo to Hoover, January 16 1935, BKF #3872

[149] Alt letter to Hoover, January 30 1935, BKF #4188

[150] Hoover to Tamm, January 30 1935, BKF #4312; Later on February 5, when it was discovered the Chicago office was holding $300 taken from Doc Barker, Hoover exploded: "I want it to be distinctly understood that Section 29 of the Manual of Rules and Regulations is still in force and effect... I do not know how many other instances there are of our field offices around the country holding personal property belonging to criminals. I would like to have an immediate instruction issued to all field offices and to all officials of the Division that the provisions of Section 29 are to be strictly observed." BKF #4333

[151] Tamm memo to Hoover, February 8, 1935, BKF #4454

[152] Hoover memo to Tamm, January 17 1935, BKF #3792

[153] Tamm memo to Hoover, January 17 1935, BKF #3855

[154] Connelley letter to Hoover, January 20th 1935 BKF #3856

[155] Alt letter to Hoover, January 29, 1935, BKF #4137

[156] Alt letter to Marian Bradford, January 26 1935, BKF #4117

[157] Alt letter to the Director, January 29 1935, BKF #4137

[158] Special Agent T. J. Donaghue report, BKF #4315

[159] Alt letter to Hoover, January 23 1935, BKF #3985

[160] Hoover letter to SAC Connelley, January 31 1935, BKF #3985

[161] Letter to Hoover, January 16 1935, BKF #4008

[162] In his statement of January 29, Bradford said that Adams offered him a $1,000 bill that belonged to "that son-of-a-bitch" who left here (Karpis). Bradford refused the money.

[163] Connelley report, BKF #4315

[164] Tamm memo to Hoover, Janaury 22 1935, BKF #4030

[165] Connelley letter to Hoover, February 7 1935, BKF #4416

[166] Marian Bradford letter to Hoover, February 26 1935, BKF #4961; Hoover letter to Bradford and Hoover to Alt, #4961

[167] Telegram to Hugh Cummings, January 16 1935, BKF #3927

[168] A.P. Buie letter to Hoover, January 18 1935, BKF#4550

[169] Jacksonville Times-Union, September 17 1935, BKF #7420

[1] The Alvin Karpis Story, Alvin Karpis, page 183.

[2] Ibid, page 187.